San Diego Christian College
2100 Greenfield Drive
El Cajon, CA 92019

# DEADLY
# EMOTIONS

UNDERSTAND THE MIND-BODY-SPIRIT
CONNECTION THAT CAN HEAL OR DESTROY YOU

## Don Colbert, M.D.

OLIVER
NELSON
™
THOMAS NELSON PUBLISHERS®
Nashville

A Division of Thomas Nelson, Inc.
www.ThomasNelson.com

Library of Congress Cataloging-in-Publication Data

Colbert, Don.
   Deadly emotions : understand the mind-body-spirit connection that can heal or destroy you / Don Colbert.
     p. cm.
   ISBN 0-7852-6743-3 (hardcover)
   1. Emotions—Health aspects. 2. Emotions—Religious aspects. 3. Mind and body. I. Title.
   RC455.4.E46C64 2003
   613—dc22

                                   2003016083

*Printed in the United States of America*

03 04 05 06 07 BVG 5 4 3 2 1

To my partner in life, my wife Mary.
A very special "thank you" for your valuable insight and
participation in all of my work,
and for your love and continued support.
You are simply wonderful!

And to my parents,
who walked with me through my early years
sharing their wisdom and love.
Thanks for helping me to discover and
work on my own "emotions."
I will be forever grateful to you both.

# CONTENTS

CONTENTS

# FOREWORD

Dr. Don Colbert is one of the most remarkable men I know. He is a skilled medical doctor, but he's more than that. He is a strong believer in and follower of Christ Jesus. He knows medicine, but he also knows the Lord—and very importantly, he understands people. He understands that God created us as *whole* human beings—body, mind, emotions, and spirit.

Dr. Colbert's basic message is one we all need to hear, and especially hear in the Christian community: What we feel emotionally often becomes HOW we feel physically.

I have talked with and counseled hundreds of people through the years, and I am keenly aware of the devastating consequences of "dis-ease" in the human heart. Dis-ease is emotional and spiritual discomfort. It is disharmony of the soul. It is often related to plaguing doubts, painful memories, hurtful stress, unforgiveness towards others, and unforgiven sins. Literally millions of people in our world today are suffering from dis-ease.

What I have also come to see is that dis-ease seems to produce disease in the body. When the mind, heart, and spirit aren't fully whole, how can the body be fully well?

Not all disease is caused by dis-ease of the soul and spirit, but a good percentage of it is. We need to recognize this truth so we can deal with the emotions that damage us—and in some cases, destroy us—as human beings.

As a physician, Dr. Colbert approaches this subject from a slightly different perspective than a pastor or spiritual counselor. He begins, as most physicians do, with the diagnosis of the problem. It's tough to hear a diagnosis, especially one with potentially grave consequences. It's tough for some people to face the reality of the mind-body connection. In fact, it can be discouraging or depressing—a real "downer"—to hear a diagnosis that puts some of the responsibility for wholeness on the individual, rather than on a virus, bacteria, or genetic predisposition. As difficult as a diagnosis may be to hear, an accurate and full diagnosis is critical if a person, and his or her physician, is going to get to the root of a problem so it can be remedied!

The first part of Dr. Colbert's book is a diagnosis. The last part is a prescription. The prescription holds out the hope of a positive, health-producing approach to a joyful and healthy life. Dr. Colbert challenges us individually to make serious choices—to choose to think and feel differently, to choose to forgive, to choose love, and throughout, to choose to trust God, who created us and desires to heal us.

I strongly encourage you to read all of this book, and to take it to heart. Do what it says to do, and don't delay in it. What you read here could extend your life and increase your quality of life. It could even save your life.

Always bear in mind that God's desire for you *is wholeness*. The phrase used repeatedly by Jesus was, "Be thou made *whole*." Wholeness encompasses *all* that we are as human beings—it includes our mind and emotions as well as our spirit and physical body as we surrender our will to do the will of God.

Seek wholeness. Ask God for it. Pursue it diligently.

What you seek . . . the Bible promises you will find.

What you ask God for . . . the Bible promises He will grant.

What you pursue diligently . . . the Bible promises you will have.

BILL BRIGHT
Founder of Campus Crusade for Christ, International

# INTRODUCTION

## Isn't Anyone Happy Anymore?

My wife, Mary, and I recently had dinner with a longtime friend and surgeon. Clark is a rising star in the medical profession, good-looking, wealthy, and a great deal of fun to be around. He has been searching for a wife for nearly twenty years. Since my wife and I agree that most women would classify Clark as quite a catch, I asked why he hadn't found someone. Clark's response astonished me.

He told us that he dates women frequently, but the relationships always seem to end the same way. He said, "All the women I meet don't just have emotional baggage—they have *cargo*!"

Clark, who loves to laugh and enjoy life to the fullest, seems to find himself repeatedly in relationships with women whose lives are entrenched in deeply toxic emotions: resentment and bitterness (often in the aftermath of a divorce), anxiety and fear owing to past experiences, depression, grief, gloom, and despair. After Clark had told us of several experiences, he held his arms up over his black curly hair and boomed out in his deep voice, "Isn't anyone happy anymore?" Wow. It was a good question.

Later that evening, Mary and I tried to list the names of individuals we believe are genuinely happy. The list was pitifully short.

As a nation, we in the United States of America consume five billion tranquilizers, five billion barbiturates, three billion amphetamines, and sixteen thousand tons of aspirin *every year*.[1] And that's barely the tip of the iceberg of medications and substances such as alcohol, nicotine, and various other stimulants we take each year in an attempt to cope with toxic emotions and their resulting stress.

Unfortunately, these medications and treatments don't seem to be stemming the tide. Studies are linking more and more modern diseases to an epidemic of deadly emotions in our culture. Heart disease, hypertension, strokes, incidences of cancer, ulcers, skin diseases, and headaches all seem to be on the rise, in spite of decades of research and innovative treatments to treat these diseases once we diagnose them. We have done very little to get to the *core* of disease or to prevent it.

## UNPACKING THE CARGO

Over the years, I have worked with thousands of patients whose doctors have diagnosed them with incurable diseases such as late-stage cancer and with those who have suffered massive heart attacks. Their primary-care physicians have told a significant number of these patients they have three to six months to live. For most of these patients, their diagnosis or heart attack was a major wake-up call for them to deal with not only their physical health, but also their emotional health and relationships.

Without fail, the first thing these patients choose to do is to stop devoting as much of their time and energy to emotional issues that are painful to them. Rather, they focus on what is truly important in their lives: God, love of family, forgiveness, and other aspects of life that bring them deep peace and happiness. A death sentence has a way of clarifying a person's values.

Why do we have to suffer before we begin to seek genuine emotional health and inner peace? Surely there must be a better way!

As I have talked with these patients, I have come to the conclusion that a high percentage of people in our world seem to approach their lives a little like they approach a roller-coaster ride at an amusement park. They allow their lives to happen to them. They strap themselves in and with grim determination, they hang on during the ups, downs, excitement, and fear. They don't even know how much stress they are internalizing. The longer the ride lasts, the more accustomed they become to the knots in their stomachs and the tension in their necks. In like manner, the longer a person approaches life as a stress-laden ride that he cannot avoid, the more accustomed that person gets to guzzling the Maalox or popping the Prozac—until he reaches the point where disappointment, pain, worry, fear, anger, bitterness, resentment, and varying degrees of the "blues" just seem to be the norm of life.

We seem to have forgotten that there *might* be a different way to live . . . at least until a physician says with sadness, "Your time on this earth appears to be running out."

I don't know about you, but when I get off a roller-coaster ride, I sometimes feel a little wobbly in the knees—especially if that roller coaster is one of the new high-speed, loop-the-loop coasters with a vertical-drop G-force that truly stresses the body.

An emotional roller coaster can also render a person a little wobbly—unsure, unstable, stressed-out, weak, and incapable of full functioning. Emotional roller coasters sap a person of both physical and psychological health, often leaving both mind and body depleted of energy and strength.

The medical facts seem to multiply every year:

- The mind and body are linked. How you feel emotionally can determine how you feel physically.

- Certain emotions release hormones into the physical body that, in turn, can trigger the development of a host of diseases.

- Researchers have directly and scientifically linked emotions to hypertension, cardiovascular disease, and diseases related to the immune system. Studies have also highly correlated emotions with infections, allergies, and autoimmune diseases.

- Specifically, research has linked emotions such as depression to an increased risk of developing cancer and heart disease.

Emotions such as anxiety and fear have shown a direct tie to heart palpitations, mitral valve prolapse, irritable bowel syndrome, and tension headaches, as well as other diseases.

Is there any good news on this bleak horizon?
Absolutely!

The good news is that you can do a great deal to pull the plug on these toxic emotions that fuel deadly and painful diseases. You can do much to improve your physical health by addressing first and foremost your emotional health.

My message is one of encouragement for you today. It *is* possible to be genuinely *happy!* And it's possible without the use of man-made chemicals, medications, and mood-altering substances.

It *is* possible to prevent many of the diseases we dread, starting with emotional health.

It *is* possible to live a vibrant, pain-free, and disease-free life— in body, mind, and spirit!

# Part I

# THE DIAGNOSIS

## UNDERSTANDING DAMAGING EMOTIONS

# ─┤ 1 ├─

# *WHAT* YOU FEEL EMOTIONALLY BECOMES *HOW* YOU FEEL PHYSICALLY

A friend of mine—in good health, I hasten to add—once said to me, "After my husband left me, I was heartbroken. I truly had meant my vows and I was ready to tough out just about anything: better or worse, richer or poorer, sickness or health. It never crossed my mind that I'd get worse, poor, and a husband who was emotionally sick all at once in the first two years of our marriage."

My friend continued, "Shortly after Todd left, my friend Ellen came to me and said something that I thought was strange. She said, 'Really take care of your health, Jess. Do the right things. Don't get sick.'

"Other people had come to me during that time to tell me I needed to get into therapy, pray more, laugh more, go out with friends more, join this club or that club, or do various other things to get over my heartache. Ellen came to me with words about my physical health and she caught me off guard.

"I asked, 'What do you mean?' She said, 'I know you're doing the right things mentally and emotionally. Just keep exercising and getting enough rest and eating the right things. You've got to build up your strength and energy.'

"I had to admit that she might be making a good point. In the weeks after the divorce, I found myself sleeping a lot—more than usual and maybe even more than necessary. I didn't seem to have as much

3

strength or energy as I had enjoyed just a few months before. I pressed her further, 'Why are you saying this to me? What do you know that I need to know?' She said, 'Jess, I've seen a lot of people get sick after they get divorced.' I knew Ellen was a nurse. I asked, 'You see them in the hospital?' She replied, 'Or in the funeral home. I know of at least two dozen people who developed very serious diseases two to five years after their divorces. At least nine of those people have died.'

"Ellen got my attention," my friend Jess concluded. "I made a decision that very day that I was going to do everything in my power to stop wallowing in my heartache and to start building strength and energy. I started on a very serious health program of exercise, eating the right foods, and taking time to rest and have fun with friends. I also started on a serious program of spiritual renewal. I stayed well. In fact, I became stronger and more energetic and more productive than I was before my wedding."

Jess put into words what many physicians know intuitively. Through the years we physicians frequently see patients go through emotionally devastating experiences such as divorce, bankruptcy, or the death of a child—only to see those patients experience heart attacks, recurrences of cancer, autoimmune disease, or serious crippling or disabling conditions.

As physicians, however, the vast majority of us have been trained to separate emotions from physical disease. Our training teaches us that emotions are . . . well, emotional. Diseases are strictly physical.

Increasingly, however, we are having to confront the fact that the *body* cannot differentiate between stress that physical factors cause and stress that emotional factors cause. Stress is stress. And the consequences of too much unmediated stress are the same regardless of the factors that led to a buildup.

## HOW WAS YOUR YESTERDAY?

I recently asked a patient, "Describe what you experienced yesterday. Don't just tell me what you did, but *who* said what and *who* did what to you or with you."

4

Ben suffered from chronic migraine headaches but the main reason he came to me was because he had just learned he had very serious cardiovascular risk factors—his primary-care physician had told him that he was a "heart attack waiting to happen."

Here is a summary of what Ben shared with me:

- He sat in bumper-to-bumper traffic going to work, which made him late for an important meeting even though he had left home earlier than usual.

- He sat in bumper-to-bumper traffic on the way home. His wife was upset when he arrived because the meal she had prepared was cold.

- While in the car, he listened to a deejay on the radio who hosted a talk show for people who seemed especially angry or prone to argument.

- He opened the mail to find an insufficient-funds notice related to his college-age daughter's checking account, and two past-due credit-card bills that he thought he had paid.

- His teenage son arrived home sullen and sulking. It finally dawned on Ben that he had failed to show up for his son's baseball game yet again, even though Ben had promised his son he would be there. His son had hit a home run but didn't seem all that eager to share any details.

- His ten-year-old daughter refused to do her homework. In picking up a pile of papers she had left out on the dining table, Ben found that on two of the spelling tests she had earned D grades.

- A clerk had given him incorrect change and refused to admit his mistake.

- He had stood in a "ten items or less" line for fifteen minutes because the cash register broke. All of the other lines in the store were even longer.

- His wife was exhausted from a day of car trouble, an unpleasant encounter with their daughter's soccer coach, and a pile of laundry that she had to do so their son would have a clean uniform for the next day's game.

- He had turned on the TV to try to unwind, only to hear reports about a serial killer loose in his city, the arrest of a corrupt county politician, and another loss on Wall Street that he knew meant a negative hit to his retirement fund.

- The child living next door didn't seem to be able to practice his saxophone without squeaking. And there was no way he could face yet another encounter with the child's father, who refused to shut the child's bedroom window.

When Ben finished his litany of "yesterday," I realized that I was feeling more tense than when Ben had walked into my office! I could only imagine how much tension had built up in him after living through such a day.

"Was this a pretty typical day?" I asked.

"Yeah," he said. "Actually it was easier than most days. I thought it was a pretty good one."

"Don't you feel stressed-out?" I asked.

"Oh, sure," he said. "But doesn't everybody?"

"Not everybody," I said. "But just about everybody. The goal here is to help you not be like 'everybody.'"

Ben, unfortunately, *is* the norm in our culture. According to the American Institute of Stress, between 75 and 90 percent of all visits to primary-care physicians result from *stress-related disorders*.[1] But the treatment for stress is usually very superficial, medically speaking.

BETWEEN 75 AND 90 PERCENT OF ALL VISITS TO
PRIMARY-CARE PHYSICIANS RESULT FROM
*STRESS-RELATED DISORDERS.*

## PULLING OUT THE WEED BY ITS ROOTS

Most of us have done our share of Saturday morning mowing and weeding. We have learned that it doesn't pay just to snap off the top of a dandelion or a clump of crabgrass. To do so seems to ensure another bountiful crop of these annoying weeds.

When it comes to treating certain physical symptoms, we often just take off the top of the symptom. We do what we can to get rid of the immediate pain or to settle the immediate upset stomach. The problem comes back . . . we take the pills or liquid or powdery medication once again . . . the problem comes back . . . we take another round of treatment . . . and so forth, week after week, month after month, year after year.

That's the usual approach. The first outcropping of stress tends to be in the form of tension headaches, digestive-tract problems (stomach, intestines, bowels), and skin eruptions. These conditions, of course, just add another layer of stress.

If we don't treat the core stress, the symptoms may become chronic. New, deeper symptoms can also arise: sleeplessness; weight loss or gain; muscle aches, especially back and leg pain; general lethargy or feelings of exhaustion; sluggish thinking; and lack of get-up-and-go or ambition. Our general response seems to be to pop a few more pills, try another diet, exercise for a few days and then give up, and berate ourselves not only for our lack of fitness and health but for our inability to stick with a good health program. All the while, we've added yet another layer of stressors to the mix.

If we continue to ignore the core stress, the symptoms can become outright disease—the kinds that require surgery, chemotherapy and radiation therapy, heavy-duty medications, and other serious treatment protocols. Each of these treatments, of course, is also a stress-producer! So is the diagnosis of a major life-altering or life-shortening disease.

Stress upon stress upon stress upon stress; and all the while, the body doesn't differentiate what caused the stress in the first place:

- The little arguments and sniping that led to full-blown marital disagreement

- The constant inhaling of toxic chemicals at the factory

- The increasingly frequent nightmares of abusive experiences in early childhood

- The inhaling or ingestion of carcinogenic substances over time

- The nearly constant feelings of frustration at the ineptness and stupidity of just about everybody encountered in life

- The decades of eating chemically laden luncheon meats and hydrogenated fats

- The flashback memories of horrific accidents or war scenes

- The inability ever to get on top of the deadlines related to an overbooked schedule and overloaded job description

No, the body doesn't know or care *what* caused the stress. All the body knows is that it is experiencing stress.

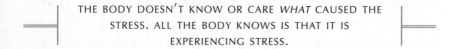

THE BODY DOESN'T KNOW OR CARE *WHAT* CAUSED THE STRESS. ALL THE BODY KNOWS IS THAT IT IS EXPERIENCING STRESS.

## STRESS, STRESS, AND MORE STRESS

*Stress* is mental or physical tension, strain, or pressure. I like the spin stress researchers and authors Doc Childre and Howard Martin give this definition:

Stress is the body and mind's response to any pressure that disrupts their normal balance. It occurs when our perceptions of events don't meet our expectations *and we don't manage our reaction to the disappointment.* Stress—that unmanaged reac-

8

tion—expresses itself as resistance, tension, strain, or frustration, throwing off our physiological and psychological equilibrium and keeping us out of sync. If our equilibrium is disturbed for long, the stress becomes disabling. We fade from overload, feel emotionally shut down, and eventually get sick.[2]

Stress reactions are the ways in which our bodies process and release both the emotions and the negative physical elements we experience in life.

Dr. Candace Pert, a stress-research pioneer, has said, "In the beginning of my work, I matter-of-factly presumed that emotions were in the head or the brain. Now I would say they are really in the body."[3]

No person experiences an emotion just in his "heart" or in his "mind." Rather, a person experiences an emotion in the form of chemical reactions in the *body* and the *brain*. These chemical reactions occur at both the organ level—stomach, heart, large muscles, and so forth—and at the *cellular* level.

## THE SCIENTIFIC LINK GROWS STRONGER

Through the years, the scientific studies linking the emotions and disease have produced an impressive body of research, all of which points to the conclusion that *what* we feel as emotions results in *how* we feel physically. Let me share just a few highlights from research in the last fifteen years:

- In a ten-year study, individuals who could not manage their emotional stress had a 40 percent higher death rate than nonstressed individuals.[4]

- A Harvard Medical School study of 1,623 heart-attack survivors concluded that anger brought on by emotional conflicts doubled the risk of subsequent heart attacks compared to those who remained calm.[5]

- The Harvard School of Public Health conducted a twenty-year study that involved more than seventeen hundred older men. The study found that the men who worried about social conditions, health, and personal finances had a significantly increased risk of coronary heart disease.[6]

- A study of 202 professional women found that tension between career and personal commitment to spouse, children, and friends was a factor associated with heart disease in women.[7]

- An international study of 2,829 people between the ages of fifty-five and eighty-five found that individuals who reported the highest levels of personal "mastery"—feelings of control over life events—had a nearly 60 percent lower risk of death compared with those who felt relatively helpless in the face of life's challenges.[8]

- A heart disease study at the Mayo Clinic found that psychological stress was the strongest predictor of future cardiac events, including cardiac death, cardiac arrest, and heart attack.[9]

Just how does emotion produce a physical manifestation? We turn there next.

# 2

# THE PATH FROM DAMAGING
# EMOTION TO DEADLY DISEASE

Why did I get this disease?" Jim said with a grilling tone to his voice. "Huh? You docs seem to know so much—why did I get this?"

Most of the patients I see are more sad than mad the first time I meet them. Jim was mad.

"You're angry that you were given this diagnosis, aren't you?" I asked. "You're angry you have this disease, aren't you?"

"You bet I am!" Jim bellowed. "I've done everything I know to live a good life. I have worked hard, been faithful to my wife, and tried to do the right thing. I don't deserve this."

"Do you think life has treated you as fairly as you've treated life?" I asked.

"Not at all! Ever since I was a kid, life has been throwing up hurdles. It's been one thing after the next. I finally decided I'd learn to get over those hurdles rather than fall into them or trip over them. Up goes a hurdle . . . Jim goes over it . . . up goes another hurdle . . . Jim goes over it. I've deserved a little of what's come my way, but trust me, Doc, *most* of what has come my way hasn't been my doing. Now here's a hurdle that Jim is being told he just may not be able to get over."

Jim and I talked for nearly an hour. He had been an attorney for thirty-eight years and like many attorneys, he was looking for someone to blame—not necessarily someone to sue, but someone or some cause that would allow him to classify and define the enemy. It was important to his sense of justice to have a defendant so he could prosecute that defendant for the crime of his ill health.

"I think you need to take a look, Jim, at the way you have *felt* about the obstacles and hurdles in your life," I finally said. After a little more discussion, Jim suddenly stood up, and with his jaw jutting in my direction said, "What? Are you telling me that I may be responsible for this disease? Let me tell you, Doc, I don't believe in emotions. I don't have many and the few I've got, I learned not to show 'em."

"You're showing one right now," I said. "The bottom line, Jim, is this: Do you want to get well? Do you really want to get across this hurdle and live to see another one?"

Jim slumped back into his chair. "Yes," he said quietly. "I do. I'm not ready to pack it in yet. But before you tell me what to do, I need to know why you think emotions have any part in this."

He gave me an open door to answer the question: How can emotions turn into physical disease?

## HOW EMOTIONS TURN INTO DISEASE

We can sum up in one word the basic communication link between what we think in the brain and what we experience in the cells of the body: *neuropeptides*. Now, before your eyes glaze over and you assume that I'm going to assault you with a lot of medical mumbo jumbo, let me assure you that I'm going to describe the physical process of how emotions turn into disease in very simple terms. Those of you who are physicians or medical researchers may find this explanation overly simplified, but I ask for your patience.

Dr. Candace Pert, a noted stress researcher, demonstrated that a certain class of our immune cells—the *monocytes*—have tiny molecules on their surface called *neuroreceptors* that are a perfect fit for neuropeptides. All of the monocytes have these receptor sites.

The brain produces the neuropeptides—which are chains of amino acids—and conducts them along the nervous cells throughout the body. They are like the keys that fit into the molecular locks of every cell of the body. Dr. Pert has called them "bits of brain floating through the body."[1] The brain "talks" to the immune cells all over the body, and in turn, the immune system cells communicate back to the brain, using these messengers called neuropeptides.[2] If your brain interprets physical perceptions as anger, fear, or depression, every immune cell of your body knows that interpretation very quickly!

IF YOUR BRAIN INTERPRETS PHYSICAL PERCEPTIONS AS ANGER, FEAR, OR DEPRESSION, EVERY IMMUNE CELL OF YOUR BODY KNOWS THAT INTERPRETATION VERY QUICKLY!

Not only do the brain and the cells of the body communicate, but the cells of the body also have a degree of memory. Thousands of people have watched the progress the well-known actor Christopher Reeve has made. A fall from a horse left Reeve paralyzed years ago. Since that time, he has undergone extensive physical therapy, with other people pushing, pulling, and manipulating his legs and arms into positions that are normal for a feeling person. As old cells in these muscles, nerves, and tissues have died and been replaced, the new cells do not appear to have a memory of paralysis but rather, a memory associated with the motion that was exerted upon the old cells. They display a willingness to be moved. The memory of how these cells, tissues, nerves, and muscles are *supposed* to move has been transferred from one set of cells that were manipulated to another set of cells that are awaiting manipulation! The memory is not in the brain, but in the cells of the body.

Stress reactions at the cellular level are pervasive and far-reaching. Fear, for example, triggers more than fourteen hundred known physical and chemical stress reactions and activates more than thirty different hormones and neurotransmitters.[3]

Back in the 1920s, Dr. Walter Cannon, a physiologist, was the first to describe what he called the *fight-or-flight response* as a part of stress reaction. Many consider him the grandfather of stress research. In May 1936, Dr. Cannon wrote an article titled "The Role of Emotion in Disease," which the *Annals of Internal Medicine* published. He stated that when an individual saw himself under extreme attack, the fear released in response to that perception would cause significant physiological changes in the body. Strong fear produced a signal that the body needed to defend itself or run away.[4]

An entire system of physical responses involves primarily the hormones epinephrine and norepinephrine. These two hormones have a dramatic effect on the sympathetic nervous system during periods of intense stress.

When a stressful event occurs, the brain perceives the stress and responds by triggering the release of specific hormones from the hypothalamus, pituitary gland, and adrenal gland. The stress response also triggers the adrenal glands to release epinephrine, which is also called adrenaline. The sympathetic nerves are stimulated to release more epinephrine throughout the body. The sympathetic nerves are located throughout the body, even in our organs and tissues, so when they are stimulated, your heart rate increases, your colon is stimulated (which may cause diarrhea), you sweat, your bronchial tubes dilate allowing more oxygen to enter, and so on.

## KEEPING THE HORMONES IN BALANCE

Hormones work in a very precise balance in the body. The right amount of any one hormone produces positive results. Too much or too little of a particular hormone, however, can produce negative results.

Dr. Hans Selye, an endocrinologist, was one of the first researchers to link emotional stress and disease. He reasoned that fear, anger, and other stressful emotions caused the adrenal glands to become enlarged by overstimulating the pituitary gland. In other words, too much stress causes the pituitary gland to produce an *oversupply* of hormones.[5]

We've all heard stories about a little old woman lifting a car off a young child who has become trapped under it, or the enraged soldier who takes on an entire enemy battalion by himself. That rush of adrenaline during high stress can enable the body to perform amazing feats of strength.

## THE TRICKY CHARACTER OF ADRENALINE

Adrenaline is a stress hormone that produces a high as powerful as that of any drug. Elevated levels of adrenaline can make a person feel *great*. The person who has adrenaline pumping through his body has a lot of energy, needs less sleep, and tends to feel very excited about life in general. Many professionals who enjoy the high-stress demands of their professions can become addicted to stress—actually, they are addicted to their own flow of adrenaline. Executives climbing the corporate ladder, attorneys battling in the courtroom, and ER physicians who handle one major trauma after another have all reported addictions to adrenaline.[6]

> MANY PROFESSIONALS WHO ENJOY THE HIGH-STRESS
> DEMANDS OF THEIR PROFESSIONS CAN BECOME
> ADDICTED TO STRESS.

Adrenaline is a powerful hormone that has far-reaching physical effects. It focuses the brain, sharpens eyesight, and contracts muscles in preparation of fight or flight. It also causes blood pressure and heart rate to increase, even as blood vessels constrict. When adrenaline begins to flow through the body, digestion shuts down as blood is shunted away from the digestive tract and sent to the muscles.

When stress is short-lived, a little burst of adrenaline does more good than harm. For example, if a person finds himself facing an angry pit bull, or a sudden assault from an enraged person, the body will likely react to the perceived danger and stress by pumping a burst of adrenaline and cortisol into the system. This burst is followed by fatigue and a need to rest. Most people know that after a particularly frightful or angry encounter, they feel exhausted. They need to take a breather.

Bear in mind that the body also perceives a fight with a spouse or teenager, or an anger response when someone cuts you off in traffic, as also needing a little burst of adrenaline and cortisol. As I stated before, the body doesn't differentiate what *causes* the need for a little extra hormone. It perceives danger or difficulty and responds quickly.

In normal conditions, this cycle of adrenaline/cortisol and fatigue/rest in response to short-term stress is generally harmless to the body. And it can potentially save your life, for example, by enabling you to fight an angry pit bull or run fast to safety.

Long-term stress, however, can keep the stress hormones pumping into a person's system on a nearly constant basis. For example, if a person is living for years in a state of unresolved anger toward a spouse or child, the flow of adrenaline can become excessive. Or if a person works for years under a boss or system that makes her feel powerless and abused, that person may experience nearly constant anger or a sense of danger. This long-term emotional stress causes a steady flow of the hormones adrenaline and cortisol into the bloodstream, and that flow has a very damaging effect on the body.

Prolonged, elevated levels of adrenaline may increase heart rate and blood pressure to the point that a rapid heartbeat and high blood pressure become the norm. That's not good.

Elevated levels of adrenaline over time can also cause an elevation in triglycerides, which are fats in the blood, and elevation of blood sugar. This also is not good.

And elevated levels of adrenaline over time can also cause blood to clot faster (which contributes to plaquing), the thyroid to become overly stimulated, and the body to produce more cholesterol. All of these effects are potentially deadly over time.

## WHAT ABOUT EXCESSIVE CORTISOL?

I've mentioned that when the body releases adrenaline into the system, it also releases a hormone called cortisol.

Elevated levels of cortisol over time cause blood sugar levels and insulin levels to rise and remain at higher levels. Triglycerides increase in the bloodstream and can stay at elevated levels. Cholesterol levels can also rise and remain at high levels. Too much cortisol can also make the body gain weight and retain weight, especially in the midsection of the body.

Too much cortisol in the body can deplete bones of vital calcium, magnesium, and potassium. It can lead to bone loss. In addition, too much cortisol can cause the body to retain sodium (salt), which contributes to increases in blood pressure.

Chronically elevated levels of cortisol have been shown to:

- Impair immune function—and a faulty immune response has been linked to a wide range of diseases.[7]

- Reduce glucose utilization—a major factor in both diabetes and weight control.[8]

- Increase bone loss—which has implications for osteoporosis.[9]

- Reduce muscle mass and inhibit skin growth and regeneration—both of which are directly related to strength, weight control, and the general aging process.[10]

- Increase fat accumulation.[11]

- Impair memory and learning and destroy brain cells.[12]

## TOO MUCH FOR TOO LONG

If left unchecked, the perpetual release of the stress hormones adrenaline and cortisol can sear the body in a way that is similar to acid searing metal. Even hours after any immediate stress-producing incident has subsided, these hormone levels can remain high and continue to do their damaging work.

THE PERPETUAL RELEASE OF THE STRESS HORMONES ADRENALINE AND CORTISOL CAN SEAR THE BODY IN A WAY THAT IS SIMILAR TO ACID SEARING METAL.

When long-term emotional stress continues and reaches the *chronic* level, the results of the continual production of these hormones become even more destructive. This is when toxic emotions become *deadly* emotions. The body begins to damage itself. This powerful ongoing infusion of chemicals injures tissues and organs, and the result can take many different disease forms.

The sad fact is that, as a nation, we are starting out on the overstressed track at younger and younger ages. In his book *The Pleasure Prescription*, Paul Pearsall contends that young people today are stressed-out even before they get a chance to start out. He relates a discussion with one of his college students:

> "I'm always one of two ways," said an honor student in my psychology class. "I'm either tired and bored or stressed and maxed out. I only have two gears, high and low, and I think I must have burned out my clutch. What worries me most is that nothing seems really wonderful anymore. I don't get really excited or really sad. I hardly ever have a good, long laugh or even a nice, cleansing cry. I'm going through the motions but I just don't seem to have emotions. I've been to Disneyland and Disney World. I've jet-skied, bungee-jumped, had wild sex, been drunk out of my mind, and on drugs. Nothing turns me on or off. I'm only nineteen years old—I feel like I'm in a pre-life crisis."[13]

Pearsall concluded in the aftermath of this conversation that many of his students displayed classic symptoms of burnout and stage-three stress exhaustion. He wrote: "They come to class looking tired, coughing, sneezing, and suffering from all sorts of infections from chronic colds to mononucleosis. When I ask what they do for fun, the most frequent response is 'hang.' When I ask what they mean by that, they answer, 'just hang around looking for something to happen to turn them on.'"[14]

By the time the average young person in our culture reaches adulthood, he or she has witnessed more than seventy thousand simulated murders on television.[15] The mind of a child does not differentiate simulated murders from those that are real. The mind perceives danger and responds to danger. We all know that feeling we get while watching a particularly suspenseful or frightening movie. The body experiences a momentary adrenaline response. The same thing can happen if we perceive a wad of lint as being a spider: the adrenaline flows even if the spider is only imaginary. The same is true for a child witnessing potentially deadly events. The stimulation is there—even if the event isn't *really* there.

Seeking *pleasure* through external stimulation can be just as much a fast track to stress addiction as messages that are frightening or gruesome. The body internalizes the stimulation of the new perception as stress, and the stress hormones end up working in the body like any other drug, creating a natural high in response to the new experience. It's that good feeling hormones cause that makes us interpret the event as thrilling or exciting.

An ongoing craving for this hormone-created high produces what some call an *urgency response,* which is a state of dependence on stress neurohormones. This happens when a person continually seeks something new, unusual, innovative, or sensory-compelling. Such a person races from one high-drama experience to the next. The result is that the person comes to consider overstimulation the norm and anything less than that hormone rush a boring letdown.

Adrenaline eventually becomes addictive. Just as an alcoholic must have alcohol, an adrenaline addict is physically and psychologically addicted to a regular dose of adrenaline. And just as is the case in most other chemical dependencies, adrenaline addiction is extremely destructive to the body. The person who comes off an adrenaline addiction usually has severe withdrawal symptoms.

## TWO KEY PRINCIPLES RELATED TO STRESS

We need to understand clearly that the body perceives stress created by good experiences in the same way it perceives stress created by negative experiences. We also need to understand the following principles:

*Principle #1: Not All Stress Is Equal*

Certain emotional states are much more damaging than others. Extreme joy and extreme sorrow both exert physical stress. But intense grief is far more damaging than intense joy! We have something of a stress gauge in our bodies. The emotions that are most damaging are rage, unforgiveness, depression, anger, worry, frustration, fear, grief, and guilt.

*Principle #2: We Need to Learn How to Turn Off Stress*

We also must understand that stress hormones become elevated in the body when a person is unable to turn off a stress response. A stress response is good only if one experiences it over the short term. Chronic stress response is *always* negative in the long run of life.

# 3

# TURN OFF THE STRESS HORMONES!

I will never forget the words of one psychiatry professor in medical school. He had previously been a dermatologist for a number of years and had treated countless psoriasis sufferers. On one particular occasion I approached him and asked why he left the field of dermatology to study psychiatry. He told me that his work as a dermatologist had led him to conclude that many individuals who were suffering with psoriasis and eczema were actually "weeping through their skin." In other words, these people for one reason or another were unable to weep openly, even though they had experienced events that warranted a good cry. They were releasing their sorrow through their skin, where it manifested itself in painful or irritating rashes.

Research has shown that outbreaks of psoriasis and eczema increase when a person is under stress. Eczema has actually been called a "boiling" of the skin. Stress worsens eczema.

If your body could talk, it no doubt would tell you through a skin disorder, "I can't take any more of these stress-producing emotions!"

Even though I am not a dermatologist, my advice to you is to pay attention when your skin starts to cry. As a physician, my strong admonition to you is this: learn to turn off stress!

## WHAT'S YOUR PERCEPTION?

Stress is not about events and experiences nearly so much as it is about a person's *perception* of the circumstances that occur in his or her life. A person's stress level has to do with what a person *believes*.

Let me explain a little further.

What one person may consider stressful, another person may not find stressful at all. One person may take planning a dinner party for forty people totally in stride, enjoying all aspects of the planning process as well as hosting the event itself. Another person may absolutely panic at the idea of giving an informal dinner party for six people.

Is there something inherently stressful about throwing a dinner party? No. Is there something inherently harmful about the number of people invited to a dinner party, or whether the party is formal or informal? No.

The difference in whether the event is stressful or not lies in the *perception*—it lies in what the individual *believes* to be the importance of the event, the potential consequences of the event, and the amount of effort associated with the event.

A person recently said to me, "I don't get it. On Friday, I get up absolutely exhausted and I go through my day in great anticipation that the weekend is coming. I collapse into bed at night, grateful I can sleep in and don't have to go to work the next day. But then on Saturday morning I awaken *earlier* than I do on a workday. I dive into projects around the house and then do a round of shopping errands, perhaps taking time out for morning coffee with a friend and then going to a late-afternoon movie and dinner with friends. At the end of the day I've accomplished just as much or more than I do on a workday, I'm just as much on the go, I talk to just as many people and get just as many or more tasks done, and I'm not at all tired at the end of the day. What's with that?"

I said, "You don't believe Saturday is a *work*day. It's all about perception. You perceive Monday, Tuesday, Wednesday, Thursday, and Friday as being about work, and you believe work means effort, responsibility, a tight schedule, intense focus, and all kinds of other things that you perceive are difficult. You perceive that Saturday is about play, and you believe play means fun, friends, shopping, and 'playing house.' What you believe, what you perceive, determines how much stress you have, and the amount of stress determines how tired you feel at the end of the day."

A man once told me that he could play a professional football game and not feel any stress—he was sore at the end of the game but not particularly tired—but that an hour of paying bills totally did him in to the point that he needed a nap. Was bill-paying more physically stressful than playing football? No. This man perceived football as fun and exciting. He believed bill-paying was boring and difficult. What he believed about each activity determined the stress he experienced in each activity.

When it comes to stress, *believing* is key.

New York psychiatrists Dr. Thomas Holmes and Dr. Richard Rahe are two of the researchers who noted that even positive and desirable events and experiences—such as marriage or the birth of a child—can be stressful.[1] How can this be? Because of what we *believe* about the happy event.

Think about it for a minute. Were your hands shaking during your wedding ceremony? Did your knees knock together or did your mouth go dry? Were your palms sweaty?

Did you experience a little of this same emotional response the last time you were pulled over for a traffic ticket?

We've all heard stories of the person who had a heart attack after hearing that he'd won the lottery, or after hearing that a sup- posedly dead or long-lost loved one was returning home. We've all heard stories of a person who died while having sexual intercourse. Stress researcher Robert Sapolsky has written: "How can joyful experiences kill you in the same way that sudden grief does? Clearly because they share some similar traits. Extreme anger and joy have different effects on reproductive physiology, on growth, most probably on the immune system as well, but with regard to the cardiovascular system, they have fairly similar effects."[2]

This concept is at the heart of the link between the emotions we feel and how we feel physically.

## THE DEVELOPMENT OF MENTAL HABITS

Have you ever awakened thinking about a particularly painful event from the past, and then found yourself going through your morning acting as if that event had just happened the day before? Dreams often trigger memories of the past, and in many people, just remembering past hurts and wounds causes a stress response in the body.

The brain doesn't really distinguish, biochemically, whether a memory is short-term or long-term. Once the idea of a memory is released into biochemical code, the body responds to the chemicals. The body doesn't have a clue if the event is currently happening or happened fifteen years ago. Just thinking about previous deep emotional hurts can cause the body to respond as if those hurts are occurring in that very moment.

Furthermore, the longer we dwell upon old hurts and wounds over time, the more we build a mental habit into our minds so that the stress response occurs more quickly each time we allow the old emotions to resurface. The body suffers the pain of being fired, losing a promotion, or the rejection of a divorce again and again and again—in fact, every time the person vividly recalls the memory of the event and the emotions involved.

This is why it is not uncommon for an individual to develop disease months, even years, after a severe life crisis, such as being raped or losing a loved one to death.

## THE CONNECTION IS REAL

A number of people, including a number of physicians, dismiss the importance of mind-body diseases or psychosomatic ailments. Many physicians have been taught that such diseases don't really exist—they are all figments of the imagination. The truth is, they do exist. They may very well start in the imagination, or in the perceiving and believing processes in the mind—but they end up in very real physical ailments. Talk to any person who has suffered from a mind-body disease for years and he will confirm that it is just as painful and uncomfortable as any other disease; and sometimes these diseases are *more* painful and cause *more* suffering. Don't minimize a disease that has a mind-body connection. Medical research is showing more and more that there may be a mind-body connection to *most* diseases and ailments, not just a few.

> MEDICAL RESEARCH IS SHOWING MORE AND MORE THAT
> THERE MAY BE A MIND-BODY CONNECTION TO *MOST*
> DISEASES AND AILMENTS, NOT JUST A FEW.

Psychiatric diseases that have been linked to long-term stress include generalized anxiety disorder, panic attacks, post-traumatic stress disorder, depression, phobias, obsessive-compulsive disorder, as well as other more rare psychiatric diseases.

The manifestation of long-term stress may also be in the form of *physical* diseases or ailments. Playing games with chronic stress places nearly every organ system of the body at grave risk. Unmediated chronic stress has been linked to a long list of physical problems:

• Heart and Vascular Problems

> Hypertension
>
> Palpitations
>
> Arrhythmias
>
> Dizziness and lightheadedness
>
> Mitral valve prolapse (a loss of tone of the mitral valve of the heart, which may cause leakage of the valve)
>
> Paroxysmal atrial tachycardia (an arrhythmia)
>
> Premature ventricular or atrial contractions (irregular heartbeats)

• Gastrointestinal Problems

> Gastroesophogeal reflux disease

Ulcers

Gastritis

Heartburn

Indigestion

Constipation

Diarrhea and bowel irregularities

Irritable bowel syndrome

Inflammatory bowel disease (including Crohn's disease and ulcerative colitis)

• Headaches

Migraine headaches

Tension headaches

• Skin Conditions

Psoriasis

Eczema

Hives

Acne

• Genitourinary Tract

Chronic prostatitis (an infection of the prostate)

Chronic and recurrent yeast infections

Frequent urination

Loss of sex drive and impotence

Frequent urinary-tract infections

Lower progesterone and testosterone levels

- Pain and Inflammation

    Chronic back pain

    Fibromyalgia

    Chronic pain syndromes

    Tendonitis

    Carpal tunnel syndrome

    TMJ problems

- Lung and Breathing Problems

    Chronic or recurrent colds, sinus infections, sore throats, ear infections

    Chronic or recurrent bronchitis, pneumonia

    Asthma

    Bronchospasms

    Shortness of breath

    Hyperventilation

- Immune Impairment

    Chronic fatigue

    Chronic and recurring infections of all types

The immune impairment that prolonged stress causes may manifest itself in a host of other ways. It has also been linked to diseases such as mononucleosis or Epstein-Barr virus, CMV (cytomegalovirus, a type of virus), food and environmental allergies as well as autoimmune diseases such as rheumatoid arthritis, lupus, Graves' disease, and multiple sclerosis. Medical research has documented that those living with long-term stress have a higher risk of developing viral and bacterial illnesses than those who do not live with long-term stress. Their bodies are much more susceptible to developing a infection from bacteria, viruses, parasites, and fungi.

## STRESS AND SPECIFIC CONDITIONS

### The Link to Cancer

Natural "killer" cells of the immune system are the body's first line of defense against cancer cells as well as viruses, bacteria, and fungi. What few people realize is that cancer cells are common in all people. Most of us, however, have healthy immune systems that efficiently and powerfully destroy these dangerous cells. The natural "killer" cells of the immune system attack cancer cells before they can form a tumor.

The foremost means of cancer prevention is to have a strong and balanced immune system, which stress can corrupt.

### The Link to Autoimmune Diseases

Many people talk about building up their immunity, but let me emphasize balance when it comes to the immune system. The brain regulates the body's immune response and when the regulatory influence of the brain is disrupted, the result may not be a lessening of immune response (less activation of the natural "killer" cells) but an overstimulation of the immune response. In these cases, the immune system goes into overdrive—it's as if the throttle gets stuck and the system remains in perpetually high gear. The result is that the body's immune system not only turns against bacteria, viruses, parasites, fungi, and cancer cells but also against healthy cells. Eventually the result is an inflammatory autoimmune disease, such as rheumatoid arthritis or lupus.

What disrupts the regulatory influence of the brain when it comes to immunity? Chronic stress is one of the major disrupters!

### The Link to Allergies

Allergic diseases are all directly linked to the body's immune system, including allergic rhinitis, food allergies, skin rashes, eczema, and asthma. Essentially, the body's immune system becomes confused, causing a reaction to an essentially harmless substance as if it were a dangerous substance. Excessive stress can cause that confusion. The body then views allergens such as dust, animal dander, and mold as foreign invaders, and the immune system mounts an assault against them. During the attack, the white blood cells ("mast" cells) release histamines, which in turn create symptoms such as sneezing, itchy eyes, runny nose, and nasal congestion. The body is doing its best to expel the irritating item.

If the allergen is in a food or beverage, the body triggers GI tract and skin reactions in an attempt to expel the irritating substance. In its severest form, this physical response can cause an anaphylactic reaction and death—such intense reactions can result from insect stings from wasps and bees, medications such as antibiotics, and foods such as shellfish and peanuts.

### The Link to Skin Diseases

Many different studies have shown that stress, as well as other psychological factors, is associated with the onset and worsening of symptoms in patients with psoriasis.[3]

Psoriasis is like a volcano erupting from the pressure of unseen forces just below the surface of a person's life. The body is releasing fear, frustration, anger, and other toxic emotions. The painful, itchy psoriasis flare-up is a strong signal of rebellion against the level of stress the person is experiencing.

The link between acne and stress is also well documented. Stress acne occurs more often in middle-aged women climbing the corporate ladder than in any other age and social-strata group. It also occurs commonly among those who are taking final exams, those who have high-stress jobs, and those who are rushing to meet a deadline.[4]

One of the great complicating dangers of these skin reactions is this: psoriasis, eczema, and stress acne all cause a puncturing of the skin. These conditions, especially if they are in eruption stage, create small open wounds in the skin that allow microscopic organisms to enter the body. This easily can lead to infection. Infections acquired through the skin are sometimes most difficult to cure, and rarely, they can become deadly. Medical literature over the last hundred years reports a number of fatal cases of staph infections related to boils and other skin conditions, especially if the open wound was initially on the head or face. The poison of the infection in many of those cases went directly to the brain.

This is true of instances in which a third-degree burn damages the protective covering of the skin as well. All kinds of microscopic organisms have an opportunity to enter the body.

It is extremely important that you not take skin eruptions lightly.

Stress, of course, shows up in the skin in ways other than disease. Telltale features are usually etched into the face. Stress signature lines appear on the forehead and at the corners of the mouth. These lines remain even when a person is asleep.

### Other Links to Disease

Jaws stay clenched and teeth grind at night when a person is chronically stressed. Many of those who suffer with TMJ (temporomandibular joint) problems are those who are stressed-out.

In one medical research study, about 80 percent of people afflicted with multiple sclerosis reported experiencing threatening and stressful life events about a year before the onset of the disease. That was compared with only 35 to 50 percent of a control group (people without multiple sclerosis).[5]

While stress may not be a known cause of some diseases, studies have shown it to dramatically increase the pain or suffering associated with autoimmune diseases including rheumatoid arthritis, multiple sclerosis, psoriasis, and Graves' disease.[6]

## AN OVERSTUFFED CLOSET

Do you have a closet or cupboard in your home where you stash stuff in a hurry—perhaps when you are preparing for the arrival of guests or cleaning the house in anticipation of a party? Most of us have junk drawers or odds-and-ends storage areas. We store our stuff until the day comes when we can't get the drawer shut or keep the closet door closed.

The same is true for us in our emotional lives. If a person keeps stuffing toxic emotions year after year, the day *will* come when those buried emotions come pouring out.

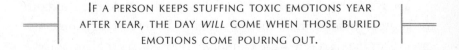

IF A PERSON KEEPS STUFFING TOXIC EMOTIONS YEAR AFTER YEAR, THE DAY *WILL* COME WHEN THOSE BURIED EMOTIONS COME POURING OUT.

The end of all stress-hormone addictions isn't beautiful and it isn't fun. The result is a state of bad health marked by a weakened immune system, heart problems, and premature aging.[7]

## THE ADDICTIVE POWER OF STRESS HORMONES

I've mentioned that adrenaline creates as powerful a high as morphine, and it affects the body chemically in much the same way, using the same receptors.

Stress hormones act a little like a carrot held out just in front of a donkey's nose. If we ever get the carrot, we feel let down. The carrot isn't nearly as satisfying as we expected, but the chase for it was invigorating. Those addicted to stress hormones don't give up the chase—it's even better than the carrot. They simply look for a new goal to pursue.

Those who are addicted to stress hormones are often very successful in their careers because they are always pushing themselves to achieve new goals or are in pursuit of a new conquest that will give them a temporary emotional high. They like the thrill of the chase, whether the chase is in pursuit of a career, lifestyle, financial goal, or some other prize.

Getting charged up at an exciting athletic event or watching an action-packed movie may be fun for the moment. But the internalization of being continually charged up can put a person on the fast track to total burnout. Remember always: the heart, nervous systems, and various other organs of the body respond to positive stress events in exactly the same way they respond to negative stress events.

Others who are addicted to stress hormones do not pursue goals, but rather seem to stay in nearly continual emotional crises. They live their lives running from one emotional catastrophe to another—the pot is always stirred up and boiling; the relationships are always marked by conflict and change; the meddling and controlling never end. Have you ever wondered why certain people just can't seem to relax—they are wound up over some problem or issue on a nearly constant basis? The reason may very well be that the person has lived at a heightened state of emotion for so long that he or she has become addicted to stress hormones.

I've witnessed families in which one teenager throws the family into a tailspin by getting pregnant. The second teenager then drops the bombshell that he's into drugs. Dad seems angry all the time and Mom is perpetually depressed. It's very possible for an entire family to live in a "state of high" levels of stress hormones—one person's stress helps create more stress for all others in the family until all are addicted to their own adrenaline and cortisol.

## GET TO THE ROOT OF THE STRESS

If you are living your life in what seems like a constant state of hurry or emergency, you may very well be addicted to your own stress hormones. You may feel good right now as you burn the candle at both ends, but remember that eventually those two burning ends will meet each other.

At the root of a stress addiction is the need to feel good, or at least to feel better. People who have this addiction become so consumed with meeting their desires to feel happy emotionally that they eventually become numb to what really matters most to them in life. You will learn how to deal with this later on in the chapters on forgiveness, distortional thinking, and love.

Stop to think for a moment about what you *really* desire. It very likely isn't material possessions, new experiences, a chemically induced high, or any other attribute often associated with a fast-lane lifestyle. I am a physician in Florida, and a significant percentage of my patients are elderly. When it comes down to the end of life, people very often get their priorities in line and start focusing on what they truly desire:

- Peace with God
- Loving family relationships and good health (marked by good energy and enduring strength)
- Peace of mind
- Joyful, simple pleasures
- Time with friends
- Having a purpose in living, usually indicated by purposeful giving to others

What people do *not* want also becomes very clear: living in an atmosphere of argument, abuse, or aggression; too-tight schedules; too many commitments, obligations, or responsibilities; exhaustion and weakness; loss of interest in living, apathy, or severe lack of ambition and goals; loss of purpose; or a life void of spirituality.

Why wait until a terminal disease diagnosis or old age to live the way you want to live? Why wait to have the emotionally satisfying and health-producing life you truly desire?

# 4

# THE WORST THINGS YOU CAN FEEL FOR YOUR HEART

Years ago a pastor came to me. Karl was on three blood-pressure medications that were not working as a treatment for his hypertension. He had been to a number of doctors, none of whom had found the key for bringing his alarmingly high blood pressure under consistent control.

Karl's condition was erratic—at times his blood pressure was normal, but in a flash it could jump off the charts, registering systolic levels over 200 (less than 140 is normal) and diastolic levels over 130 (less than 90 is normal).

In my practice, my staff and I take the time to sit down with patients such as Karl to see if there is an emotional event that might be triggering a particular illness or condition. Again and again, we've found that emotional upheaval appears to be linked directly to disease. At other times, physical factors are at the root or are part of the cause. Karl was not obese, so there was no clear-cut cause for his hypertension.

When I sat down with Karl, I questioned him specifically about events that may have been present in his life at the time his physician first diagnosed him with blood-pressure problems. He told me that he had lost his ministerial position after a particularly vicious split in the church. He left the position with enormous anger at the individuals he perceived to have seized control of the church.

I wasn't surprised at what Karl told me. Through the years, I've discovered that pastors and others in full-time Christian and charitable work often have difficulty in forgiving those they believe have hurt them or erred spiritually. Many of these individuals are deeply sensitive, caring people who are wounded deeply when they feel they have been misjudged, unfairly criticized or blamed, or falsely accused. Rather than vent the fact that they are wounded, they internalize the feelings and allow them to steep into a seething mix of anger and hostility.

I discussed with Karl his medical need to forgive those who had hurt him. I was not prepared for him to boil over in nearly instant rage. Like an erupting volcano, he let out a scream so loud the entire office heard him.

Karl's angry screams continued unbroken for quite a long time, punctuated by strong statements of hatred toward those who had "robbed" him of his church and had "demeaned" his value as a pastor. When he finally became more quiet, having fully vented his pent-up emotions for perhaps the first time since he left the pastorate several years earlier, he told me he knew that he needed to forgive and that he finally felt that he could.

Karl began to voice words of forgiveness toward the individual people he had been holding hostage in the prison of his heart. Within fifteen minutes of his doing this, his blood pressure, which had been 220/130 when he came in, plummeted to 160/100. His face, which had been almost contorted into a harsh scowl that seemed chiseled into his features, had relaxed to the point that he looked like a different man.

## WHAT'S WORTH DYING FOR?

Without a doubt, hostility, rage, and anger are at the top of the list of toxic emotions that generate an extreme stress reaction. *Hostility* is often the term we use to embody several damaging emotions. Technically, hostility is defined as a feeling of enmity, ill will, unfriendliness, etc.; antagonism.[1] It is an abiding, long-term state—something of a perpetual worldview.

A hostile person is likely to get angry and become excessively irritated over trivial circumstances that would not upset most other people. Cardiologist Dr. Robert Elliott has described the hostile person as a hot reactor who burns a dollar's worth of energy for a dime's worth of stress. He wastes five dollars' worth of energy on a two-cent problem.[2]

In 1980, Dr. Redford Williams and his colleagues at Duke University demonstrated that getting a high score on a fifty-item hostility test was positively correlated with the severity of coronary artery disease.

The hostility test used in the research is part of the MMPI (Minnesota Multiphasic Personality Inventory), a widely used psychological test first developed in the 1950s. Dr. Williams refined the test, defining three very specific categories of hostile responses: attitudes, emotions, and behavior.

The main hostile attitude he isolated was cynicism, which is a distrust of the motives of others. The main emotion he isolated was anger. The main behavior he isolated was aggression.

Aggression is a physical act, but it isn't necessarily one we would describe as violent. Aggression may be expressed subtly as a front, a sulking posture or demeanor, or an incidence of arguing.

Dr. Williams required that scores from each of these three components—attitudes, emotions, and behavior—be added together to come up with a total hostility score.[3]

Many hostile people don't believe they are angry, cynical, or aggressive. They describe themselves as "frustrated" or "strung out." Frustration, however, is very often a facet of anger, as is impatience.

The fact is, most people are angrier than they realize. Many people in our society today are angry deep within. About 20 percent of the general population have levels of hostility that are high enough to be dangerous to their health—that's one in five! Another 20 percent have very low levels of hostility, and the rest of the population falls somewhere in between.[4]

ABOUT 20 PERCENT OF THE GENERAL POPULATION HAVE
LEVELS OF HOSTILITY THAT ARE HIGH ENOUGH TO BE
DANGEROUS TO THEIR HEALTH—THAT'S ONE IN FIVE!

Anger ranges from minor annoyance to murderous rage. To uncover your own state of anger, I encourage you to take the Anger Inventory in the back of this book (Appendix B). If you find that you score average or higher, you need to take action. Your health is at risk.

## HOSTILITY AND YOUR HEART

Hostility produces very real physiological reactions in the body.

Hostile people release more adrenaline and norepinephrine into their blood than nonhostile people. In general terms, these hormones raise blood pressure by constricting blood vessels and increasing heart rate. Angry people also have elevated cortisol levels. As noted in an earlier chapter, elevated cortisol levels cause the body to retain sodium (salt), which adds to the blood-pressure problem. Elevated cortisol also raises triglycerides and cholesterol, and makes platelets stickier—all of which predispose a person to heart disease. Over time, if the hostility becomes engrained in the person's emotional identity, the blood pressure problems become more permanent.

War, one of the most stressful of all human experiences, can cause a major release of stress-reaction hormones. Autopsy studies of soldiers killed during the Korean and Vietnam Wars revealed that 75 percent of them had already developed some form of atherosclerosis at the age of twenty-five and younger. Had these young men lived, the internal emotional war zone they had experienced may very well have caused just as much damage to their cardiovascular systems as the physical war zone in which they had fought.[5]

### The Damage of High Blood Pressure

Let me give you a simple, short course on why high blood pressure is so damaging.

The coronary arteries that supply blood to the heart are probably the most stressed arteries in the entire body. Every time the heart beats, these arteries are squeezed flat, similar to a fire hose not being used. Then a blast of blood inflates them to their full capacity. This squeezing and flattening effect takes place more than a hundred thousand times in a single day.

Stress-reaction hormones affect primarily the lining of the arteries, called the *endothelium*. This lining is made of a single layer of cells (endothelial cells) and looks similar to the inner lining of a garden hose. The single layer of cells is tough, but it can become damaged if too much pressure is placed on the vessel wall. When that happens, white blood cells, cholesterol, and platelets rush in to repair the damage. The repair "patch" creates what is called atherosclerotic plaquing. Since the coronary arteries supply the blood for the heart, which never stops working, it is these arteries that often show the most plaquing. Microscopic particles of LDL (bad) cholesterol can also pass into the artery wall, where they become oxidized and cause even more plaque to form.

As time goes on, collagen fibers and smooth muscle cells may move into this area of repair and trap fibrin (a protein important in clotting), calcium, and other minerals. All of these reactions cause the arterial wall to thicken and eventually bulge into the central opening (lumen) of the artery.

Fatty plaques lining the coronary arteries can rupture. When the plaque bursts, sticky platelets clump up and pack against the ruptured plaque. This ball of gluey blood and fat gets larger and larger, a little like a snowball growing in size as it rolls down the side of a hill. Eventually this ball of blood and fat can become so large that it blocks the vessel, or it can break loose and move into a narrower part of the vessel and block the vessel at that point. The result is a heart attack.

What happens in times of stress? Adrenaline is released into the bloodstream, causing the heart to speed up and beat harder. Adrenaline is also triggering the coronary arteries and the heart to dilate in an effort to deliver more oxygen and nutrients to the heart muscle. If the coronary arteries are filled with plaque, or if the coronary arterial walls have been thickened owing to high blood-pressure damage, then instead of dilating, the coronary arteries constrict.

Imagine your heart pumping hard and fast, struggling to supply the heart's and brain's demands for increasing amounts of oxygen and glucose. But instead of the coronary arteries dilating or opening up as they should, they constrict. The heart then must beat even harder and faster. The harder and faster the beating, the greater the constriction! The end result is angina, a heart attack, arrhythmia, or the release of a blood clot that results in total blockage of a key vessel and sudden death.

## THE DISEASE CONSEQUENCES OF
## UNCHECKED HOSTILITY

Numerous medical and scientific studies have linked anger, rage, hostility, and associated emotions with heart disease. Let me summarize a few of these findings for you.

- A study done in Finland showed that hostility is a major risk factor and predictor of coronary artery disease. A nine-year population-based study done as a follow-up to this study revealed that high-hostility scorers were almost three times more likely to die from cardiovascular disease than low scorers.[6]

- Hostility may actually be a better predictor of coronary disease risk than the standard risk factors of cigarette smoking, high blood pressure, and high cholesterol. Approximately 800 men took part in the study, and the average age was sixty when their level of hostility was measured by a hostility questionnaire. Forty-five percent of the participants reported at least one heart-related event in the three years of follow-up. The men who scored highest on the hostility test were the ones most likely to suffer heart problems, according to researchers.[7]

- Ichiro Kawachi, of the Harvard School of Public Health, also has reported studies that link anger and coronary heart disease. He has written, "The relative risk of heart attack among angry patients looks as strong as it is for hypertension or smoking. Clinicians should screen their patients for a history of anger, and consider referring them to counseling or anger management therapy."[8]

- Other medical researchers have also reported this link. In fact, a recently reported study has indicated that hostility poses a greater risk of heart disease than either smoking or high cholesterol. In this particular study of 774 men, average age sixty, the researchers took a look at all the traditional heart disease risk factors: smoking, high cholesterol, waist-to-hip ratio, alcohol consumption, poor socioeconomic factors, and hostility. They found that among the men with a high level of hostility, nearly 6 percent experienced at least one cardiac event during the study (such as a heart attack or hospital admission for heart problems). This percentage of cardiac incidents was significantly higher than the rate of heart problems associated with any other risk factor.[9]

REFUSING TO DEAL WITH PENT-UP RAGE MAY OPEN THE DOOR TO EARLY DEATH.

- Refusing to deal with pent-up rage may open the door to early death. In a twenty-five-year follow-up study involving 255 University of North Carolina medical students, Dr. John Barefoot—now at Duke University—found that those who scored highest in hostility on a standard personality test were nearly five times as likely to die of heart disease as their less hostile classmates. They were seven times more likely to die by the age of fifty.[10]

- In a similar study conducted among law students, those with the highest levels of hostility had more than a fourfold risk of dying within the next twenty-five years.[11]

## DO YOU HAVE PENT-UP HOSTILITY?

Dr. Elliott uses several tests to determine if people are "hot reactors"—those who usually have chronic hostility and erratic high blood pressure. He has people play video games and perform mental arithmetic, such as subtracting mentally by sevens, starting at 777. He also has the participants perform a cold-pressure test, which involves placing their hands in ice water for seventy seconds. If blood pressure rises dramatically during these tests, there's a high probability the particular person is a "hot reactor."[12]

In my practice, I have found that most people who have hostility *know* it deep down inside; they just call what they feel different names. Some tell me they have a "short fuse" or a "quick temper."

Others tell me that they are highly motivated and therefore are very "impatient." A constant state of frustration is actually a subtle form of hostility rooted in anger at other people, at situations, and at circumstances.

Still others tell me that they periodically fly off the handle but that they cool off just as quickly as they heat up. Later, they'll tell me about problems that always seem to trigger their outbursts of anger. They often are similar or repeated events that have the same hallmarks. That's hostility! Their hostility tends to go back to one—or perhaps a few—instances that occurred in the past, sometimes many years before or even in childhood.

Hostile people internalize or bury their anger. They create a pressure-cooker environment for themselves, much like what Karl developed. We need to remember that no particular experience or event is automatically a hostility producer. Karl, for example, may very well have been the only person who came away from the church split feeling hostility. For others, that event in the church may have brought relief or joy. Again, it's a matter of perception, belief, and internalization.

## ARE YOU A PRESSURE-COOKER PERSON?

Various studies have shown that people with high hostility also tend to exhibit two major types of behavior.

### 1. Overindulgent Behavior

High-hostility scorers tend to be smokers, drinkers, and overeaters. They also tend to have higher cholesterol levels. In other words, not only does their hostility give them a bent toward heart disease, but their hostility may drive them to behaviors that also contribute to heart disease![13] This is a real double whammy.

The hostile person who turns to nicotine to calm down, to food for comfort, or to alcohol for relaxation is a person who is not truly addressing the toxic emotion at the root of his life. He is only compounding the consequences associated with the toxic emotion.

### 2. Type A Personality Behavior

About fifty years ago, San Francisco cardiologists Meyer Friedman and Ray Rosenman introduced the phrase "type A personality" to our cultural vocabulary. They characterized the type A person as being impatient, extremely competitive, always in a hurry, and chronically angry and hostile. They also described them as being highly aggressive, ambitious, and hardworking, easily irritated by delays and interruptions. They often have difficulty relaxing without feeling guilty, tend to finish other people's sentences for them, and are easily frustrated. People with this personality are likely to honk their car horns and fume in traffic jams, bark at slow-moving clerks in stores, and feel compelled to do two or three things at once (multitask), such as talk on the phone while shaving or driving.

Dr. Friedman described himself as a type A person who had suffered a heart attack at an early age. After linking his personality with his brush with death, Dr. Friedman modified his lifestyle and attitude. He died at the age of ninety in April of 2001. When he was eighty-six, he was still running the Meyer Friedman Institute at the University of California at San Francisco.

Friedman and Rosenman actually discovered the type A behavior by accident after they realized that their waiting-room chairs needed to be reupholstered much sooner than anticipated. When the upholsterer arrived to do the work, he carefully inspected the chairs and noted that the upholstery had worn in an unusual way. He had never seen this pattern of wear in other physicians' waiting rooms. The front few inches of the seat cushions, as well as the front portions of the armrests, were prematurely worn while the back areas of the chairs were not. The usual pattern was for the backs of chairs to wear out first. He concluded that the people in the chairs were anxiously sitting on the edge of their seats, likely holding on to the edges of their armrests as they nervously awaited being called into an examining room. As they squirmed and fidgeted, they wore out the upholstery. They showed classic type A personalities.

Friedman and Rosenman began researching the behavior and writing about the link between heart disease and type A personality throughout the 1950s. In 1975 they published a follow-up study of three thousand healthy men to determine if those with type A behavioral patterns tended to develop a higher incidence of coronary disease. The study lasted eight and a half years and they found that *twice* as many type A men developed coronary artery disease as their less driven type B counterparts.

Friedman and Rosenman also found that type B personalities could be pushed into type A behavior if they were given too many responsibilities and too great a job pressure. Urban life—with its deadlines, traffic, financial pressures, and so forth—tended to press people into type A behavior even if they did not have a natural predisposition to that personality.[14]

## CHECK YOUR HEART FOR THE *REAL* YOU

I encourage you to try a little exercise. Close your eyes and point to yourself. Now open them. Did you point to your head, where your brain is, or did you point to your heart? Try this with several other people. Invariably you will see that no one points to his brain, foot, or face. When you point to the real *you*, you point to your heart.

None of the ancient peoples, including people in Bible times, considered the "seat" of a man to be the brain. To the Greeks and writers of the Bible, the seat of a man's identity was in the heart— the soul, the emotions, the will, the feelings of a person.

Jesus taught, "A good man out of the good treasure of his heart brings forth good things, and an evil man out of the evil treasure brings forth evil things" (Matt. 12:35). The Bible also tells us:

> "I will put a new spirit within them, and take the stony heart out of their flesh, and give them a heart of flesh, that they may walk in My statutes and keep My judgments and do them; and they shall be My people, and I will be their God. But as for those whose hearts follow the desire for their detestable things and their abominations, I will recompense their deeds on their own heads," says the Lord GOD. (Ezek. 11:19–21)

The following verses depict the heart as capable of thinking, feeling, remembering, and prompting outward behavior:

- A merry heart makes a cheerful countenance,
     But by sorrow of the heart the spirit is broken.
     (Prov. 15:13)

- The heart of him who has understanding seeks knowledge.
     (Prov. 15:14)

- The heart of the wise teaches his mouth,
     And adds learning to his lips. (Prov. 16:23)

Your body is the living reality of everything you are, and everything you experience happens to all of you, not just to your brain. We live with a sense of condescension toward ancient people who believed the heart could think. The Bible, however, says, "As he thinks in his heart, so is he" (Prov. 23:7) and "Out of the abundance of the heart the mouth speaks" (Matt. 12:34).

> YOUR BODY IS THE LIVING REALITY OF EVERYTHING YOU ARE, AND EVERYTHING YOU EXPERIENCE HAPPENS TO ALL OF YOU, NOT JUST TO YOUR BRAIN.

"But," you may be wondering, "does my physical heart really think and feel? Isn't my heart just a physical pump?" Author and scientist Paul Pearsall described an incident that occurred when he was speaking to an international group of psychologists, psychiatrists, and social workers in Houston, Texas. He was talking about his belief in the central role of the heart in both physical and spiritual life. A physician came up to the microphone to share her story, sobbing as she did so. This is what she told Dr. Pearsall and the others present in that auditorium:

> I have a patient, an eight-year-old little girl who received the heart of a murdered ten-year-old girl. Her mother brought her to me when she started screaming at night about her dreams of the man who had murdered her donor. She said her daughter knows who it was. After several sessions, I just could not deny the reality of what this child was telling me. Her mother and I finally decided to call the police and, using the descriptions from the little girl, they found the murderer. He was easily convicted with the evidence my patient provided. The time, the weapon, the place, the clothes he wore, what the little girl he killed had said to him . . . everything the little heart transplant recipient reported was completely accurate.[15]

## THE HUMAN HEART—THE SPIRITUAL HEART

Thousands of years ago the Bible warned that sin, such as unrelenting rage and hostility, will harden the human heart. In truth, hardened or calcified arteries can leave a human heart actually looking as hard as a stone in an autopsy. "Hardness of heart" is not just a euphemism for stubbornness or a rigid attitude. It is a physical state of the heart that occurs from severe atherosclerosis. Those who have this condition usually suffer from angina, which is chest pain with physical exertion. A heart hardened by years of emotional pain and the resulting ravaging effects of stress hormones is a heart that experiences physical pain.

Can it be that the pain suffered during an acute heart attack or some other form of heart disease is the consequence of the buried pain of hidden sin, unforgiven and unrepented-of anger, unhealed abandonment, and other toxic emotions? It may very well be that the emotionally and spiritually pained heart is finally revealing its anguish in the vessels and tissues of the physical heart.

Can it be that the human physical heart is merely a reflection of what is happening to the spiritual heart? I believe it is so. We too often think that the physical reality determines the unseen reality of the soul, mind, and emotions. The Bible tells us the exact opposite process is in effect. The unseen reality of our souls, minds, and emotions is what determines the physical reality we perceive with our senses.

Regardless of which comes first—physical response or emotional response—the two work together. The physical, emotional, and spiritual are linked in ways we are only beginning to explore and understand.

# 5

# OUCH! THE LINK BETWEEN
# RAGE AND PAIN

Kelley came to me after seeing three general-practice physi-cians, an internist, and two chiropractors. She had an appointment with a pain specialist the next month. Her prob-lem: intense back pain and various other pains that seemed to roam randomly in her body—one day her head, the next day her stomach.

"There's hardly a day goes by that I don't have pretty bad pain somewhere," she told me. "I'm only forty-six years old and that doesn't seem normal."

I assured her that "pretty bad pain somewhere" isn't normal at any age.

I asked Kelley when the severe pain seemed to start. She said, "About four years ago."

I asked her to tell me about her life and her family, especially in the last five to seven years. "They've been the toughest years of my life," she said.

Kelley went on to give me a little summary of her adult life. She and her husband, Will, had married while they were sophomores in college. They had both worked and studied for the next three years and had graduated—Kelley with a degree in early childhood edu-cation and Will with a degree in graphic art. Both got jobs and in the year after they graduated, Kelley had their first child. They had another baby two years later. In the next twenty years, they moved three times, to three different states, as Will pursued better jobs. Kelley was always able to find work.

Then about five years ago the bottom seemed to drop out of their financial life. With one child in college and another nearing high school graduation, Will lost his job and then lost his next job and the next—in all, he had gone through five jobs in four years. "He just couldn't seem to hold on to anything," Kelley said. "In those four years, he only worked for nineteen months. All of the earning of the family income fell on my shoulders. That was a lot of pressure, especially on a preschool teacher's salary."

"Did your relationship with Will suffer?" I asked.

"Sure," she replied. "I tried to be supportive. Then I began to hear little comments around the edges about Will being too arrogant and too unstable and too undependable on the job. I knew Will had always had those tendencies, but they suddenly seemed out of control. I felt really angry that he was sabotaging not only his own career but also our family finances and our children's futures. I felt angry that he wouldn't face up to any of these job changes as being remotely his fault.

"I felt angry that he was putting the entire pressure and responsibility for our family income on me. He could tell I was upset and frustrated with him, although I never really yelled at him. In fact, we never really talked about how I felt—I think he knew I was angry but he pretty much felt that was my baggage to carry and that it had nothing to do with him."

"Did anything change?" I asked.

"Well, he finally got a job—not in graphic art—and has kept it. Our daughter dropped out of college for a year to work. Our son went to a community college instead of to the college he really wanted to attend. I think I'm still a little angry that Will's inability to keep a job impacted both of their lives in what I think are negative ways."

Then Kelley asked, "But what could all of this have to do with my back pain?" A lot.

## AT THE ROOT OF PAIN

Hostility and anger are directly related to pain in a number of people. We shouldn't be surprised at that. The Bible has told us this for several thousand years:

> For You have filled me with indignation.
> Why is my pain perpetual
> And my wound incurable? (Jer. 15:17–18)

> Many a time they have afflicted me from my youth;
> Yet they have not prevailed against me.
> The plowers plowed on my back;
> They made their furrows long. (Ps. 129:2–3)

Indignation, of course, is a form of anger, albeit righteous anger. To afflict, according to *Miriam Webster's Collegiate Dictionary, 10th ed.*, means "to distress so severely as to cause persistent suffering or anguish." The emotional attacks against the psalmist directly caused a painful effect on his back—such pain that it felt as if someone were plowing his back like a field.

But what about the science linking the toxic emotions of hostility or anger with pain? Dr. John Sarno, a professor of clinical rehabilitative medicine at New York University School of Medicine, has treated thousands of patients with back pain. In the early 1970s, Sarno began questioning popular diagnoses and treatments for back pain. He wondered why it was that the level of pain in an individual, and the findings of his physical exams, didn't seem to match up. At times, his findings suggested that structural abnormalities—even herniated disks—had little or nothing to do with how much pain a person reported experiencing.

Sarno began to question his patients with chronic back pain and discovered that a whopping 88 percent of them had a history of tension-induced reactions. The back-pain sufferers also tended to experience the following:

- Tension headaches

- Migraine headaches

- Eczema

- Colitis

- Ulcers

- Asthma

- Hay fever

- Frequent urination

- Irritable bowel syndrome

Dr. Sarno concluded that painful back spasms and chronic back pain often resulted from chronic tension, stress, frustrations, anxiety, repressed anger, and worry. He theorized that tension impacted blood circulation to the back muscles. Tension caused the blood vessels supplying the back muscles and nerves to constrict, thus reducing the blood supply and oxygen to the tissues. The result was painful spasms. This condition may eventually lead to numbness, the sensation of "pins and needles," and even decreased strength in the muscles.

The chronic ongoing constriction of the blood vessels produced another negative consequence: an accumulation of metabolic waste in the muscles. One of the jobs of the circulation system in the body is to carry waste products from the cells and tissues to the excretory organs, especially the kidneys and bowels but also the skin. When blood vessels are constricted, waste products back up, filling muscle tissue with metabolic waste.

The lower back is not the only area affected. The muscles of the neck, shoulders, buttocks, arms, and legs may also be impacted. The result may lead to a diagnosis of fibromyalgia, fibrositis, myofascitis, repetitive stress injury, and other conditions. Dr. Sarno named this condition of chronic pain *Tension Myositis Syndrome* or TMS.

Previous to his findings and naming of TMS, Dr. Sarno had

been treating his chronic back-pain patients according to whether their pain was related to a herniated disc, arthritis, and so forth. Overall, many of his patients had shown relatively little improvement, which is not uncommon for people with chronic back pain. Many people who suffer from back pain will tell you that they have had the condition for ten, twenty, even thirty years or longer, even though they have undergone repeated treatments and therapies. Improvement seems temporary at best in many cases.

After Dr. Sarno conducted his research, he began to treat the underlying emotional components related to TMS as well as any structural abnormalities. His patients suddenly began to improve dramatically. He experienced an astonishing success rate, with more than 90 percent of his patients reporting they were totally pain-free. In addition, between 90 and 95 percent of Dr. Sarno's patients were cured permanently, meaning they very rarely developed recurrent back pain.[1]

I frequently recommend Dr. Sarno's books—*The Mind-Body Prescription, Healing Back Pain,* and *Mind over Back Pain*—to people who come to me with chronic back pain.

## EMOTIONAL PAIN CAN PRODUCE PHYSICAL PAIN

When we speak of a person who is troublesome, irritating, annoying, or emotionally painful to us, we sometimes call that person a "pain in the neck."

When we break off a relationship with someone we dearly love, or when we have great sorrow over a loss, we often say we experience "heartache."

When someone rejects us, criticizes us, or angers us, we sometimes say the person "hurt" us.

In truth, he or she did!

But what kind of emotional pain truly becomes a lingering physical ailment? It is emotional pain that a person has suppressed.

Many parents tell their children that it is wrong for them to fully express their emotions. The kids hear that "boys don't cry" or that girls shouldn't be "crybabies." They understand that the expression of emotions is impolite to others. In some cases, parents punish children for expressing their emotions, even when the children express those emotions in appropriate ways for appropriate reasons. In addition, psychiatric studies have shown that children who experience a lack of approval and respect for their feelings when they are very young automatically develop a tendency to suppress emotions. When these young children feel their parents, teachers, coaches, siblings, or others in authority don't value what they think or feel, they tend to shut down their own value of their own emotions.

## THE BIBLE ADDRESSES ANGER

The Bible has a number of passages that directly deal with anger. One of the foremost verses speaks to the fact that we need to deal quickly with those issues and situations that cause us to feel anger, rather than to stuff our feelings inside: "'Be angry, and do not sin': do not let the sun go down on your wrath" (Eph. 4:26; see also Ps. 4:4).

Nothing is wrong with the emotion of anger per se. What is damaging is how we express our anger—for example, in violent actions against another person, causing injury to property, and so forth. What is also damaging is hanging on to anger and allowing it to build up inside us until we live in continual rage.

Jesus taught, "You have heard that it was said to those of old, 'You shall not murder, and whoever murders will be in danger of the judgment.' But I say to you that whoever is angry with his brother without a cause shall be in danger of the judgment. And whoever says to his brother, 'Raca!' shall be in danger of the council" (Matt. 5:21–22). Jesus was equating an abiding attitude of rage—the seething hostility that would murder if the opportunity arose—to an actual deed of murder. To Him, this abiding anger in a person was just as spiritually damaging as an outward murderous deed. People always spoke the word *Raca* in anger; verbal expressions of anger can be just as harmful as physical acts of violence against a person.

The truth is, we often react to words and to the attitude we perceive in others in a way that is identical to the way we'd react if that person hit us with a fist. The old adage "Sticks and stones may break my bones, but words will never hurt me" simply isn't true. Words can have a devastating emotional impact on a person.

## TEMPORARY OR PERMANENT REPRESSION

Repressing certain emotions can be healthy *in the short term*. And repressing an automatic response can give a person a little extra time in dealing with emotions that might completely overwhelm him if he experiences them all at once.

This especially happens when a loved one dies. Have you ever noticed that a bereaved family sometimes seems to hold up better than others around them during the death of a loved one? What has happened is that their minds have repressed or blocked overwhelming grief responses for a short period. Grief-stricken people may experience this state of denial for several days or even weeks until their emotions have a chance to catch up to the reality of their loss. This is a normal, healthy defensive action of the mind.

What is not healthy is for a person to bury or deny unpleasant, overwhelming emotions indefinitely—emotions that would be far healthier for the person to confront and work through. When we pretend that all is well when all is *not* well, when we tell ourselves and others that nothing bad has happened when something very bad has happened,when we act as if we have suffered no loss or pain when we have suffered great loss or pain, it is then that we are stuffing what we should express. When a person begins to pack powerful and devastating emotions into the closet of his soul, he is setting himself up for trouble.

Through the years, many people become experts at *not* feeling what they feel. They become pros at pushing down any feelings that are painful or that others do not accept.

What happens when we do this—when we hold in expressions of frustration, anger, or rejection, refuse to cry, or to voice our inner pain? Our minds perceive that we are experiencing *danger.* The negative emotions we are feeling, which cause us pain, become emotions we try to avoid or reject. A negative cycle begins. The more we experience negative emotions and fail to express them, the more the pressure inside us builds, the more our minds perceive that we are in a dangerous situation, the more we feel we should flee (shutting down our emotions further) or fight (railing against the emotions). The result can be an inner rage, fear, or anxiety that boils just below the surface of expression for years or decades.

WHEN A PERSON BEGINS TO PACK POWERFUL AND DEVASTATING EMOTIONS INTO THE CLOSET OF HIS SOUL, HE IS SETTING HIMSELF UP FOR TROUBLE.

The initial process of learning to stuff an emotion is conscious. A child has to fight back being scared or holding back tears when someone insults him. Over time, the process of stuffing emotions becomes a subconscious act—it takes less effort and is almost an automatic instinctual response to anything negative.

The Bible encourages us to "be renewed in the spirit of your mind . . . put on the new man which was created according to God, in true righteousness and holiness" (Eph. 4:23–24). The "spirit of the mind" is the subconscious—the part of your thinking that is more directly involved with your soul and spirit. Repressed, blocked emotions occur automatically in our subconscious, and very often we aren't consciously aware of them. This is the area that needs spiritual renewal. I will discuss this later, in the chapters on forgiveness, love, replacing distortional thinking, and joy.

## SIGNS OF STUFFED EMOTIONS

"But," you may be asking, "if the stuffing of emotions is largely subconscious, how can I tell if I'm doing it?"

I have seen a number of psychological tendencies in my patients apart from the manifestation of pain. People who have stuffed emotional responses from childhood or for a significant length of time tend to express one or more of the following:

*Perfectionism*

Those who stuff emotions try to keep everything "perfect" in their lives so there will be no cause for them to experience rejection, failure, or criticism.

*A Desire for Control*

Those who stuff emotions very often attempt to control every aspect of their lives—and the lives of others around them—so that no stray emotion has an opportunity to erupt or display itself.

*Self-Doubt and Self-Deprecation*

People who have stuffed emotions very often have grown up in environments in which they have felt unloved or rejected as children. In some way, they have not experienced the security and bonding of a normal parent-child relationship. As a result, they have developed low self-esteem and feelings of low self-worth, even though they may have achieved a great deal later in life.

This deeply seated low self-esteem tends to manifest itself in self-doubt—for example, second-guessing of decisions, a tendency to avoid making decisions or setting specific goals, a dissatisfaction with choices made in the past to the point that the person refuses to make future choices.

Others who have low self-worth engage in self-deprecation—they ridicule their own flaws, shrug off compliments, and make overly critical comments about their own minor failures, flaws, or errors. They are likely to be people who will instinctively respond to a new idea or situation with an "I don't know," "I'm not sure about this," or "I'm not sure that's a good idea" even before they have fully heard the idea or explored the possibilities of the new situation. In meeting new people or encountering new circumstances, they may suddenly become uncharacteristically shy or retiring.

## Cynicism and Criticism

Those who have stuffed emotions sometimes take the tack of averting attention away from themselves and onto others to avoid any further rejection, hurt, or emotional distress. They can become masterful at making cynical comments or leveling criticism at others.

## Promiscuity

This response may seem odd at the outset, but many people with low self-worth and stuffed emotions try very hard to please everyone and to seek expressions of affection in unlikely places and from unlikely people. They may become overtly promiscuous in their desire to experience the affection and security they didn't have as children, or to compensate for the rejection they felt from a former spouse.

## A "Bursting" of Emotion
Ask yourself:

- Do I seem to have an exaggerated response to very simple, everyday occurrences? Does a song suddenly bring a flood of tears? Does the scent of a particular perfume stir up a host of confused emotions?

- Do I have flashback memories or nightmares about traumatic events in the past, such as a divorce or an act of abuse?

- Do I have a strong emotional reaction to the sight of a person across a room, or perhaps a photo (even a photo of an inanimate object)?

Be aware that when these memories and reactions trigger a stress response, they may be trying to tell you something.

One of my patients shared with me how angry she felt every time she smelled peppermint. Christmas was a very difficult time for her—Christmas and candy canes and the aroma of peppermint were all intertwined. Why was this so? As she told me about her life, she revealed that her uncle had regularly molested her. During these sexual attacks, which always seemed to happen in his living room, she would look away, staring at a jar of peppermints that sat on the table next to the couch. It was little wonder to me that the smell of peppermint stirred up deep anger, resentment, and bitterness in her.

## THE STRONGER THE EMOTION, THE MORE POWERFUL THE EXPLOSION!

One of the things that those who have studied mind-body relationships have discovered is that the stronger the emotion a person stuffs, the more powerful or explosive the eventual release of that emotion later in time.

Repressed rage or extreme anger sometimes escapes the unconscious mind like a criminal fleeing from a jail cell. But terrible childhood traumas, including sexual, physical, and emotional abuse, public humiliation, and severe rejection, are all experiences that can cause an inner rage and pain that explode in sometimes violent ways later in life—sometimes in expressions of abuse against others, sometimes in crippling nightmares and an inability to sleep, sometimes in a torrent of seemingly unending tears, sometimes in various acts we as a culture describe as insanity: raging screams, self-flagellation, and so forth.

What other types of experiences create emotions that people tend to stuff?

Here are several of the foremost:

- A parent's depression or prolonged physical illness. This gives a child a feeling of insecurity, fear, and sometimes deep anger that the parent isn't providing what the child needs.

- Circumstances that produce great anxiety. These include war and graphic talk or images of war, violence, and terrorism; divorce and marital separation; extreme poverty; moving frequently. Again, a child tends to perceive these circumstances as creating an environment that is unstable, insecure, fearful, and he may feel anger that the parent or parents aren't supplying all that he needs.

- Alcoholism or drug addiction. Again, a child may internalize the addiction of a parent as creating an insecure, fearful environment.

- Extreme rigidity, strictness, or lack of affection. A child may perceive that a parent is rejecting or unfairly judging him or her. Anger can result.

Emotions that become trapped inside a person seek resolution and expression. That's part of the nature of emotions—they are meant to be felt and expressed. When we refuse to let them out, emotions just try harder. The unconscious mind has to work ever more furiously to keep the feelings under wrap.

Emotions do not die. We bury them, but we are burying something that is still living. It's a little like filling a pitcher with water. We pour cupful after cupful of negative emotion into the jar until finally the pitcher is at the overflow point. Even a slightly negative experience can be just enough to cause the pitcher to overflow.

EMOTIONS DO NOT DIE. WE BURY THEM, BUT WE ARE BURYING SOMETHING THAT IS STILL LIVING.

Those who have stuffed negative emotions, especially anger and hostility for years, don't need much to set them off. The least little insult—the driver on the freeway who cuts him off, the person at work who voices criticism her way, a person who ignores his presence—can produce an outburst that is above and beyond a normal response.

What happens in normal expressions of small amounts of anger or fear? The facial muscles tense; the entire body may feel stiff even to the point of temporary paralysis. The normal physical response to anger or fear is a tightening of the body—everything within the person prepares to flee or fight back. When we are hurt, we say "ouch"—we express the pain.

What happens when we repress anger and fear? We feel that normal tension, but the tension is turned inward instead of outward. The body transfers it to inner muscle groups. The "ouch" goes unexpressed . . . for a while. Eventually, we awaken with that stiff back or that painful neck and the "ouch" has an outlet for expression.

## ANGER IS A CONDITIONED RESPONSE

How does anger become an automatic response that flows out of our subconscious minds? This happens because we *learn* anger through repeated exposure to certain experiences in our environment.

I find it interesting that while we often learn to repress emotions in childhood, that period is when emotion-triggering experiences bombard us. Even cartoons seem to teach children to react to life with anger and rage. The same is true for many of the cop shows on prime time. The media teaches us as Americans to react to life with a short fuse—to jump to immediate conclusions and to come up with witty retorts.

Anger is a conditioned response. We learn it through repetition and through a linking of environmental cues. Dr. Ivan Pavlov, a Russian surgeon, demonstrated that dogs could be taught to salivate at the sound of a ringing bell. Initially, each time the dogs received food, they also heard the sound of a bell. They salivated at the presence of the food initially, but over time, the association between the sound of the bell and the food was so strong and so ingrained, they would salivate when only the bell sounded. This is an example of a conditioned response.

In a very similar manner, we learn to express anger when we encounter certain stresses. The moment some people hear a loud voice, they automatically draw certain conclusions and their bodies respond in a certain way, even if the person with the loud voice isn't communicating with them.

Over time, a person doesn't even realize what it is that is triggering his anger—he is simply tensed up and ready to fight or flee at all times. One day he may find himself pouring out angry words or feeling anger if the paperboy leaves the paper on the driveway. Another day a tirade may come in the presence of an incompetent salesclerk. Another day a line that seems too long at the gas station triggers an expression of anger. Rage boils up in increasingly inappropriate ways the longer a person lives with pent-up rage. Unfortunately, hostile individuals may not even realize how inappropriate their responses really are in relation to the circumstances or situations that trigger their responses.

## TURNING ANGER UPSIDE DOWN

What can we do with anger to prevent it from turning into hostility? Perhaps the first and foremost piece of advice is found in the Bible; again, "Do not let the sun go down on your wrath" (Eph. 4:26). Deal with your anger immediately.

Apologize to others quickly.

Ask God to forgive you for your outbursts of anger . . . confess your anger to Him and receive His forgiveness quickly.

One way to temporarily control anger is by taking a "time out." Similar to a child that acts up or misbehaves, when you become angry and ready to respond in a way that you will later regret, take a "time out." Refocus and collect your thoughts, calm down, and practice deep-breathing exercises to allow you to do just that. These exercises are discussed later in the book. Take five to ten slow breaths, and with each breath say "Thank You" to remind yourself of the gift of life from God. This will diffuse your anger, because an attitude of gratitude as well as the slow, deep, abdominal breathing induces the relaxation response and turns off or turns down the stress response.

Letting go of anger quickly means swallowing your pride and saying, "God's way, not my way."

## 6

# DEPRESSION ISN'T "JUST IN YOUR HEAD"

Linda, a middle-aged woman of Greek descent, sat quietly weeping in the exam room, waiting for me to enter. As I walked into the room I could almost feel the heavy cloud of depression hanging over her. She was eager, however, to share her story with someone.

Lindie, as her friends called her, grew up in a wealthy family with all of the privileges that money and high social status offer. Her mother and father had traveled abroad for months at a time when Lindie was a child, leaving her with a maid who was authorized to provide for her physical care. The elderly maid seemed to hate Linda and to be deeply envious of her status in the community. When Lindie's parents were away, this woman brutally abused the little girl, at times forcing her tiny hands into boiling pots of water, locking her in a dark cellar for hours, slapping her, and spitting on her. The maid's own children overran the house and helped themselves to Lindie's toys and the treats her parents sent, although Lindie's parents knew about none of this.

Too young to write letters, Lindie spent many of her days yearning for her parents to return. Then, on one occasion just as Lindie was expecting her parents, the maid announced to her in a cruel way that her parents had been killed in an automobile accident. She sent Lindie to her grandmother, who loved her dearly. Sadly, Lindie's grandmother died when the young girl was eleven years old. She then was sent to live with an older sister and her sister's husband.

This uncle molested her almost nightly, threatening to strangle her in her sleep if she told anyone about the abuse.

Throughout Lindie's life, she had never disobeyed, and she had never told anyone prior to her visit in my office that day about many of the details of her sad, lonely life. She had grown up and lived with deep depression almost as long as she could remember. Somehow the darkness of the cellar where she had spent hours on end had become the dark cellar of her own soul. She hadn't dared to escape from the real cellar in her parents' home. She hardly dared to venture from the cellar that she had developed in her heart.

Lindie had not come to me for treatment of her depression. She had come to me with one of the worst cases of fibromyalgia I've ever seen. She had chronic fatigue and had gained an enormous amount of weight. She was nearly bedfast owing to high blood pressure and arthritis.

Through the years, I have come to recognize that Lindie's case is not uncommon. Depression has been called the common cold of mental illness. Depressive disorders affect a staggering nineteen million adults in the United States of America. What is equally or perhaps more alarming is that 2.5 percent of children and 8.3 percent of adolescents in the United States suffer from depression as well.[1]

DEPRESSIVE DISORDERS AFFECT A STAGGERING NINETEEN MILLION ADULTS IN THE UNITED STATES OF AMERICA.

Depression, however, is not just one condition. Depression comes in a wide variety of types and degrees of severity. It is a toxic emotional and psychological state that has very real physical manifestations.

Depressed individuals tend to have generally poor health habits, which place them at even higher risk of developing most types of disease. The lifestyle choices of the depressed person nearly always result in poor nutrition, little exercise, use of alcohol or drugs, or overuse of prescription medications. Poor sleep patterns often cause fatigue. The composite result of these bad health habits is a decreased immune function and a greater risk for developing cardiovascular diseases, diabetes, and more frequent infectious diseases.

The depressed person tends to experience severe pain. States of chronic pain—such as fibromyalgia, arthritis, degenerative disk disease, headaches, TMJ problems, tendonitis, as well as chronic pain from an accident—all appear to magnify if a person is also suffering from depression. Intensified pain, of course, can increase heart rate and blood pressure. This side effect can lead to a person's taking increased dosages of medications.[2]

## THE LINK BETWEEN DEPRESSION AND DISEASE

Medical research has well documented the link between depression and disease. Let me summarize just a few of the vast number of findings.

### Depression and Heart Disease

In one thirteen-year study, those with major depression had a four-and-a-half times greater risk of heart attack compared to those with no history of depression.[3]

Other studies have shown:

- People who experienced two or more weeks of depression were more than twice as likely to experience a heart attack when compared to those with no depression at all. Depressed individuals who did suffer a heart attack were four times more likely to die from it.[4]

- Healthy individuals with elevated depression scores had a one-and-a-half times to twofold increased risk for a first heart attack, even though they had only depressive symptoms and not full-blown clinical depression.[5]

- The higher death rate of depressed people who suffered a heart attack was not linked to habits such as smoking or lack of exercise. In other words, in this study, what mattered most in predicting the heart attack was a person's depression, not his or her smoking or exercise habits. The study showed that the part of the nervous system that regulates heart rate works differently in those who are depressed. These researchers noted a strong link between depression and heart disease.[6]

## Depression and Osteoporosis

Research is also showing that depression increases one's risk for developing osteoporosis, a thinning of the bones. Both past depression and current depression have been associated with lower bone mineral density in women.[7]

## Depression and Cancer

In recent years, strong scientific evidence also suggests that depression may be linked to the formation of some types of cancer. Medical researchers have known for some time that depression is associated with poor repair of damaged DNA, and alterations in apoptosis, or cell death—which are gateways to the development of cancer.

Let me explain a little further.

Most cancer-causing agents (carcinogens) appear to induce cancer by damaging DNA in cells and causing abnormal cell reproduction. This is why it is especially important for your body to maintain a strong ability to repair DNA and destroy damaged DNA.

Apoptosis is the process that causes abnormal cells to die and be flushed from the body. As I mentioned previously, nearly every person develops cancer cells in his or her body, but most of us do not get actual cancer because apoptosis causes those cells to be eliminated just like any other toxin or foreign substance. Apoptosis is the foremost way the body defends itself against cancer cells. Depression reduces natural killer cell activity, which makes it harder for the body to destroy or eliminate abnormal cells. Thus it indirectly affects the development of cancer cells into tumors.

In addition, stress alters natural killer cell activity, reducing the function of these cells in destroying tumor cells as well as virally infected cells. Depression and stress are closely linked.

## Depression and Suicide

Perhaps the ultimate physical malady a person can experience is suicidal death. There's no recovery or remedy for this ailment, which definitely affects both body and mind!

Depression, unfortunately, can lead to a significantly higher risk of suicidal behavior, especially, it seems, in children and adolescents. In a survey completed just a few years ago, suicide was the third leading cause of death in young people between the ages of fourteen and twenty-four. It was the fourth leading cause of death in youngsters between the ages of ten and fourteen years.[8]

Early diagnosis and treatment of depression are critical if we are to stop these rising rates of suicide in our youth. More than 90 percent of those who commit suicide have a mental disorder, most commonly depression or substance abuse. Four times as many men commit suicide as women, yet women attempt suicide two to three times more often. Perhaps the reason for this is that women usually attempt suicide with an overdose of pills, which is less likely to result in death, whereas men choose more violent means of suicide such as gunshot wounds.[9]

## A Vicious Downward Spiral

As is the case with stress and disease, depression and disease can create a downward spiral. People who suffer from illnesses such as stroke, cancer, heart disease, diabetes, or any other chronic long-term debilitating illness are more prone to becoming depressed. The depression, in turn, fuels the disease. This is one of the main reasons why so many people with chronic debilitating diseases often get worse despite taking medications that normally would help improve their conditions. The upward spiral toward health often improves dramatically if a person receives treatment for depression simultaneously with treatment for his or her disease. Both psychological or cognitive therapy and medication may be warranted.

## A VARIETY OF DISORDERS UNDER ONE LABEL

Depression comes in three basic varieties: major depressive disorder, dysthymic disorder, and bipolar disorder. How can you know if you or a loved one is suffering from one of these types of depression?

*Major Depressive Disorder*

A person is experiencing a major depressive disorder if he has *five or more* of the following symptoms over a two-week period. Please note that it's not uncommon for a person to have one or two of these symptoms for a day or two—sometimes these symptoms are related to normal blood sugar or hormonal fluctuations in the body. Those who are depressed have a lingering, prolonged *cluster* of these symptoms:

*A sad, unhappy, or discouraged mood.* The person might cry easily or feel so sad that he isn't able to cry.

*A significant change in body weight or appetite.* Most depressed individuals tend to lose weight and have very little appetite. A very small portion of those who are depressed, however, gain weight— even a great deal of weight. These individuals experience a dramatic increase in appetite.

*A feeling that nothing is fun anymore.* If a person is depressed, he may find little pleasure in activities and interests that were once enjoyable. All the zest in life appears to be gone. Hobbies aren't fun any longer, and jokes don't seem funny. Everything is boring. Even sex seems uninteresting.

*Sleep patterns change.* Depressed individuals sleep too little or too much. They often experience insomnia, may have difficulty falling asleep, or may experience early-morning awakenings—such as waking around three o'clock in the morning and finding it difficult to fall back to sleep. Others with depression sleep virtually around the clock.

*Drained of energy.* Fatigue is very common among those who are depressed.

*Difficulty concentrating.* Those who are depressed are easily distracted and have memory difficulties in remembering such things as dates, names, and phone numbers they once knew well.

*Slower mobility.* People who are depressed may walk, talk, get in and out of bed, and even get dressed slower.

*Easily agitated.* Depressed people often become irritated or agitated much more quickly compared to times when they aren't depressed.

*Pessimism.* Depressed people live under a cloud of gloom, hopelessness, and worthlessness. Guilt and negative thoughts fill their minds. The future looks only bleak to them. People who have suffered from prolonged depression report that they feel as if a "dark force is consuming the soul."

*Suicidal thoughts.* Depressed people often have suicidal thoughts or seem preoccupied with thoughts about death.

What should you do if you or a loved one is experiencing five or more of these symptoms for a two-week period? Seek help from a family physician, an internist, or a psychiatrist.

Major depressive disorder is the leading cause of disability in the United States and worldwide.[10] In a given year, 9.9 million Americans suffer from major depressive disorder.[11]

### Dysthymic Disorder

Dysthymic disorder, or dysthymia, is a less severe form of depression. It often, however, is more chronic. To be diagnosed with dysthymic disorder, an adult person must have felt depressed for at least two years. Children and adolescents must have felt depressed for one year. In addition to experiencing a depressed mood for an enduring length of time, a person must have at least two other main symptoms of depression as listed in the previous section. Those with dysthymia are more prone to experience a major depressive disorder.

Dysthymia often begins in childhood, adolescence, or early adulthood. About 10.9 million American adults suffer from it![12]

### Bipolar Disorder

Doctors previously called this form of depression *manic-depressive illness*. Individuals with bipolar disorder not only have episodes of major depression but also episodes of mania, which is a persistent elevated mood. These individuals are high on life. They can go for days on little more than one or two hours of sleep and still feel rested. Manic episodes feature racing thoughts, concentration problems, feeling easily distracted, and talking nonstop. Individuals who experience mania can have greatly inflated self-esteem and a strong desire to participate in high-risk activities just for fun, such as sky-diving. Bipolar disorder affects approximately 2.3 million American adults, or 1.2 percent of the U.S. population that are 18 or older.

## WHAT DEPRESSION IS *NOT*

Not all depression is considered a disorder. Every person goes through periodic rough times when he feels a little down about life. Perhaps an exciting job opportunity doesn't pan out, a relationship may go through a time of stretching or compromise, a child may leave home for college, or bills may pile up. There are many reasons for a person to become discouraged.

Not all "feeling blue" times turn into depression, even if those instances are periodic or fairly frequent. For example, 80 percent of women experience postpartum "blues" brought on by the hormonal changes and stress of giving birth. Only 10 percent of new mothers, however, go on to experience genuine postpartum depression.[13]

Major depression goes beyond the occasional low mood. A person who is depressed feels as if all of life has a black cloud over it—a cloud that will never lift.

So how can you know if you will experience major depression at some time in your lifetime? Are there factors that can predict a depressive disorder?

Here are some of the experiences that seem most commonly to trigger depression:

- A family history of depression
- Death of a loved one—spouse, parent, child, friend—or even a beloved pet that has been part of the family for years

- Drug and alcohol abuse

- Chronic illness or chronic pain—especially people who have cancer, stroke, heart disease, or diabetes

- Abuse as a child—abused children are also more likely to abuse drugs and alcohol

- Children of divorce—children whose parents divorce suffer from depression more than those who do not experience a divorce. They also are sadder and act out more in school. They reportedly have less zest for life, lower self-esteem, and more physical complaints. They also worry more.[14] These findings also pertain to families in which parents seem to be at war with each other, even if they don't divorce. Youngsters in these families often become highly depressed and remain depressed long after their parents stop fighting.[15]

- A life crisis, such as loss of a job, separation or divorce, a jail term, personal injury. Any severely stressful event can trigger depression.

Finally, depression is *not* something that only ungodly people experience. Some seem to believe that depression is inevitably linked with sin. Unconfessed and unrepented-of sin may cause depression at times, but sin does not cause all depression. God's people are just as prone to depression as those who don't know the Lord.

GOD'S PEOPLE ARE JUST AS PRONE TO DEPRESSION AS THOSE WHO DON'T KNOW THE LORD.

Ancient accounts of people suffering from bouts of depression abound. In the Bible, King David experienced periodic depression. He spoke intimately about his depressive episodes in the Psalms. The great prophet Elijah (1 Kings 19:4) became so depressed after winning a victory against God's enemies that he asked God to take his life. People refer to Jeremiah, who witnessed Israel's captivity by neighboring Babylon, as the "weeping prophet." In Jeremiah 8:18–9:26, he openly described his discouragement over his calling to prophesy.

The good news is that others in the Bible faced situations that might cause some people to become depressed and overcame them. One such person was Joseph, the son of Jacob. Sold into slavery by his own brothers, falsely accused and imprisoned, and forgotten by those who promised to help him, he nonetheless seemed to maintain his optimism until released (Gen. 37–45). The apostle Paul and his coevangelist Silas actually sang songs after they were unjustly imprisoned—false imprisonment is certainly a potentially depressive situation (Acts 16:25, 26)!

## GETTING TO THE BIOCHEMICAL REACTIONS OF DEPRESSION

Today's new imaging technologies allow researchers and physicians to examine the brains of living people. These techniques let a doctor view both the structure and function of the brain—making abnormalities responsible for mental disorders much more readily isolated.

Clinical neuroscientist and child-adolescent psychiatrist Dr. Daniel Amen has been using brain imaging technologies for years. He uses a high-resolution SPECT (single photon emission computerized tomography) study. This allows him to see deep into areas of the brain to witness how the brain functions, something both CT scans and MRIs are unable to do.

According to Amen, the SPECT studies reveal that when the deep limbic system is overactive, negativity or pessimism are usually evident in the patient. This overactivity is highly correlated with depression. Limbic and paralimbic areas include the hippocampus, amygdala, and entorhinal cortex portions of the brain. The hippocampus controls memory and helps the brain learn and retain information. The amygdala controls fear and anxiety.

In addition, the limbic system includes the anterior and medial nuclei of the thalamus, the medial and basal parts of the striatum, and the hypothalamus. The deep limbic system is near the center of the brain and is about the size of a walnut. Amen has found that deficiencies of the neurotransmitters norepinephrine and serotonin can cause increased metabolism in the deep limbic system.[16]

I am completely convinced that brain imaging will eventually be used to diagnose depression and other mental disorders far earlier than they are presently, and by isolating the neurotransmitters, chemicals, and hormones related to various areas of brain function we will be much better able to treat depression.

Note, however, that the deep limbic system includes the hypothalamus. This is the same organ that can become overly stimulated as part of the HPA axis described earlier. There is every indication that a hormonal link between the hypothalamus and the brain may be implicated in depression, and not just in relationship to other hormone-producing glands (such as the pituitary and adrenal glands).

If an overly active limbic system (which includes the hypothalamus) is associated with negativity and pessimism—aspects of depression—it is likely this overactivity is also owing to an overactive HPA axis.

Again, we're back to the release of stress-reaction hormones!

## CHRONIC STRESS AND DEPRESSION

Not only does depression trigger stress, but one of the most potent predictors of depression is chronic stress. Depression, disease, and stress seem to form a chain-linked cycle.

A patient named George said to me one day, "I think my job is killing me." After he described what was happening in his workplace, I was inclined to agree with him . . . literally.

George had worked in the same office for years and his supervisor had bypassed him for promotion on at least four occasions. George felt as if he were always struggling to meet impossible deadlines and please an impossible boss. When the boss told him to wear a tie to work, he started wearing one, even though he sat in a cubicle and never interacted with customers. Then his boss complained that he needed to improve his handwriting, even though he nearly always typed his memos or notes on a project. He worked to write more legibly, and the supervisor then told him that he didn't produce his reports fast enough. No matter what George tried to do, he couldn't make his boss happy.

George was struggling with chronic stress. My prescription to him: change jobs.

I have met a number of children who face this same kind of long-term protracted stress in their relationship with their parents. They rarely receive praise or positive recognition for their good behavior or the character they display. Rather, their parents continually compare them to other siblings: the older sister who got better grades or the younger brother who was more athletic. Chronic family stress can be the worst kind because a person never gets away from it. At least we can leave behind stress related to work at the end of the day. But where can a child go if Mom or Dad is forever demanding greater perfection, more effort, or higher performance?

How a person copes with chronic stress directly determines whether he will become chronically depressed.

## WOMEN AND DEPRESSION

For reasons that are still unclear, depression afflicts almost twice as many women as men. The reasons may have something to do with a hormonal imbalance that triggers stress hormones.

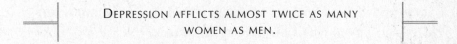

DEPRESSION AFFLICTS ALMOST TWICE AS MANY
WOMEN AS MEN.

Women are generally at greater risk after giving birth, but also at other times of hormonal fluctuation such as at menstruation and at menopause.

PMS, or premenstrual syndrome, can cause symptoms of

depression. PMS symptoms include a sad mood, loss of pleasure, decreased energy, feelings of worthlessness, sleeping problems, and concentration problems. Compare these to the symptoms of depression and you'll see a big overlap. A number of doctors treat women with PMS with antidepressant medications.

## THE HORMONE FACTOR

Just as sex hormones can play havoc with both psychological and physiological functioning (mind and body), so stress hormonal fluctuations may predispose one to or actually trigger depression.

It's the hormone factor that may very well keep some people in depressive circumstances from developing depression, while other people go immediately into depression.

The hormonal system that regulates the body's response to stress is called the HPA axis—or the hypothalamus-pituitary-adrenal axis. The hypothalamus, pituitary gland, and adrenal glands are among the foremost endocrine glands in the body. The hormones they produce work in balance with one another.

Many depressed individuals have an overactive HPA axis—they produce too much stress hormone. For those with this condition, virtually *any* long-term stressor can make them feel out of control, which can trigger depression. A stressor might be as minor as having a boss hand over a particularly difficult job or dealing with the schedules of a family of teenagers.

Feelings of being out of control can signal the body to increase the production of the CRF hormone, which the hypothalamus produces. The way the body responds is unique to each individual. Some people have such an overactive HPA axis that any threat—physical or psychological—triggers an increase of CRF production.

When CRF is increased, a series of events occur in something of an unstoppable chain reaction. First, the pituitary gland releases ACTH (hormone), which then stimulates the adrenal glands to produce more cortisol. The negative consequences of cortisol discussed in earlier chapters kick in.

Cortisol causes a person to have heightened alertness or arousal, which can interrupt sleep. Some depressed people seem to have barely enough physical energy to function, some even to the point of having difficulty in standing up. Even so, these people can have a great deal of mental energy—called a vigilant response—which can make them too alert to sleep. They end up feeling exhausted but not at all sleepy. This is a common sign of depression.

As a person becomes depressed, he feels even less in control of life. The fall down the slippery slope continues—less control triggers more CRF production, more ACTH, more cortisol, and even less control. The crash at the bottom of the slope is virtually inevitable.

We seem to be experiencing an epidemic of depression in our nation, and I believe it is directly related to this inability to shut down the stress response. A person who is prone to depression has trouble unwinding after a stressful experience. The hormones that are designed as a temporary response to stress get stuck in a revved-up pattern. Serious hormonal imbalance is likely to result, and the results are disastrous both psychologically and physically.

> WE SEEM TO BE EXPERIENCING AN EPIDEMIC OF
> DEPRESSION IN OUR NATION, AND I BELIEVE IT IS
> DIRECTLY RELATED TO THIS INABILITY TO SHUT DOWN
> THE STRESS RESPONSE.

## CUSHING'S SYNDROME

A number of years ago a physician in England, Sir Harvey Cushing, noted that some of his patients had a type of obesity that seemed different from that of the majority of his obese patients. These particular patients tended to have a very obese trunk but slender arms and legs. Some had accumulations of fat on the backs of their necks that almost gave the appearance of a buffalo hump. They had increased hair growth on their bodies, purplish stretch marks on their abdomens, and they were generally weak and fatigued. They also seemed to be discouraged and depressed.

The depression in some of Dr. Cushing's patients was so severe they actually committed suicide. When autopsies were performed on their bodies, Dr. Cushing discovered that in each case, the person had a tumor on his or her pituitary gland. This disease was named Cushing's syndrome.

Those with Cushing's displayed other serious symptoms: they often had hypertension, osteoporosis, glucose in the urine, and swelling due to water retention (edema). Women with Cushing's tended to experience the absence of a monthly menstrual period (amenorrhea).[17]

All of these symptoms are now known to be the result of too much cortisol produced by the adrenal glands. With Cushing's syndrome, the pituitary gland tumor was producing excessive amounts of ACTH. This caused the adrenal glands to produce too much cortisol. Today, we know that an increased production of cortisol is always the cause of Cushing's syndrome, even if a pituitary tumor is not present.

Studying Cushing's syndrome, researchers found that people who are depressed also have heightened levels of CRF, ACTH, and cortisol. It was an important discovery because it revealed the link between stress hormones and depression, giving psychiatrists a better handle on how to treat clinical depression.

It is reasonable to assume that if those with Cushing's syndrome were more prone to depression, all other people with elevated cortisol levels might also be prone to depression. This, however, is not necessarily the case. Only about half of those with elevated cortisol levels from causes other than Cushing's syndrome experience depression.[18]

Those patients taking high doses of Prednisone, which is a synthetic glucocorticoid (and acts as cortisone), seem to be at very high risk of developing depression.

## HELP FOR THE SEVERELY DEPRESSED

Those with more severe depression usually respond best to a combination of psychotherapy and medication. Many psychiatrists treat depression with drugs since it commonly stems from an imbalance of neurotransmitters in the brain. Antidepressant drugs influence the neurotransmitters. Older antidepressants such as MAO inhibitors and tricyclic antidepressants such as Elavil often had major side effects. Newer antidepressants, such as SSRI drugs like Prozac, Zoloft, and Paxil, produce far fewer side effects and patients are therefore much more likely to take the drugs as prescribed.

It usually takes several weeks for an antidepressant drug to relieve depression. In some cases, a combination of antidepressant medications can be helpful, especially if the person is resistant to just one antidepressant.

If a patient with severe depression doesn't respond to anti-depressants, a psychiatrist usually recommends electroconvulsive therapy (ECT), commonly known as shock treatments.[19] About 80 to 90 percent of those with very severe depression improve dramatically with ECT. This, however, is a form of therapy reserved only for severe depression that does not respond to conventional medication.

ECT, or shock treatment, in the past involved using excessive amounts of electricity, which actually caused brain damage, memory loss, convulsions, and physical injury. Now, however, ECT uses much less electricity so that there is generally no evidence of brain damage or memory loss. Individuals who have been on every known type of antidepressant and combinations of antidepressants, as well as every form of psychotherapy—and are still severely depressed— are good candidates for ECT.

## Counseling and Psychotherapy

It is interesting to me that a number of noted psychiatrists and psychologists in history started with stress-related emotions in their understanding of depression.

Sigmund Freud believed that depression was anger turned inward. He believed the anger stemmed from childhood traumas and unresolved conflicts that were hiding under many layers of defensive mechanisms such as denial.

Freud believed a person could work his way through these layers of defense mechanisms to resolve the childhood conflicts. The process of psychoanalysis he advocated involved countless hours of conversation with a trained psychiatrist.

Although some childhood traumas do predispose some individuals toward depression, the link has not always been easy to establish. The incidence of depression among children of divorced parents, especially when frequent family fighting was involved, is high. Even so, traumatic childhood events do not necessarily predestine a person to a life of depression.

Psychiatrist Dr. Aaron Beck, trained in Freudian theory, analyzed his patients' dreams to find clues to buried hostility or anger turned inward. He found, however, that dreams often represented little more than a reflection of conscious thinking or self-perceptions related to everyday life. Dr. Beck also used a standard Freudian tool called *free association* to have a patient discuss his thoughts as they occurred. Beck discovered that when his patients let their thoughts run free, they often left their supposedly therapeutic sessions feeling worse rather than better. When Beck offered patients a more practical approach to problem solving, they tended to improve very quickly. Beck eventually began working with patients to help them change or retrain their automatic or immediate thoughts. This approach became known in psychology as *cognitive therapy,* or *cognitive-behavior therapy (CBT).*

Beck eventually saw depression as a *thought disorder*—a negative way of thinking about life and circumstances—rather than anger turned inward.[20]

Cognitive therapy teaches an individual with depression how to identify and manage negative thoughts that can fuel the downward slide into depression. The cognitive therapist teaches the depressed individual to recognize which automatic thoughts or thought patterns tend to fill his mind when he feels the worst. The therapist then helps arm the sufferer with new information to contradict those negative thoughts.

I was discussing this approach one day with a colleague of mine and he gave me the example of a woman I'll call Joan. Joan was a depressed woman who believed everyone hated her. In therapy, she mentioned that her hairdresser barely spoke a word to her that morning and she convinced herself that this was a sure sign that her hairdresser was rejecting her. My friend, who is a cognitive therapist, confronted that assumption with the more probable explanation that the hairdresser was in a bad mood or perhaps had just had an argument with her boss or boyfriend.

The therapist's role is to help the patient dispute automatic thought patterns by providing evidence that contradicts the assumptions the patient is making or conclusions he is drawing. As evidence, my friend pointed out to Joan that the hairdresser had just slammed down the telephone at the time Joan arrived for her appointment.

In cognitive therapy, a patient learns to no longer accept automatic thoughts at face value. He instead dissects, examines, and questions his thoughts. The patient develops a habit of examining his thinking and questioning any negative beliefs, assumptions, or projections.

Basically, a cognitive therapist encourages an individual to distract himself from a negative thought pattern. Then the patient learns how to recognize and question old assumptions, such as "Nobody likes me." When the negative pattern is broken, the painful expectations lose their self-fulfilling power.

Cognitive therapy has produced dramatic results in cases of mild or moderate depression. Patients often experience these results in a matter of only a few weeks or months.

## LEARNED HELPLESSNESS AND INCREASED DEPRESSION

According to one study, relatives of individuals with major depression have an increased risk of approximately ten-fold for incidences of depression over the next two generations. I believe this is the result of genetics and a learning process—specifically, a "learned helplessness."[21]

As a graduate student at the University of Pennsylvania, Martin Seligman and a fellow student conducted research that showed that people learned helplessness, and therefore they could unlearn it. Seligman and his colleague took dogs that had been conditioned according to Pavlov's methods. Every day, Seligman and his associates exposed these dogs to two stimuli—a high-pitched tone and a brief shock. They expected the dogs would come to associate the tone with the shock, and therefore would react to the sound as if it were painful.

The dogs were placed in a box that had two compartments separated by a low wall, which the dogs could easily learn to jump over. To escape the shock, all the dogs had to do was jump the barrier. When exposed to the shock, however, they just lay down whimpering, and didn't even try to escape. The young researchers were baffled.

Because the dogs responded in this manner, Seligman and his colleague were unable to test their theory about the tones. The animals essentially had learned that nothing they did mattered when it came to the shock, so why try? In other words, they had learned helplessness. Seligman contends in his later writings that the animals suffering from a learned helplessness displayed many of the psychological features of depressed human beings.[22]

"Nothing good ever happens to me."

"I live under Murphy's Law—if anything can go wrong, it will."

"It's always been this way and it'll always be this way."

These and statements like them are reflections of a helpless attitude. Doctors consider these pessimistic explanations, as all statements associated with helplessness tend to be.

Seligman called making statements such as these a person's *explanatory style*, which is a rather fancy phrase for saying that they are the way a person customarily explains or interprets bad events and experiences.[23]

A person learns his explanatory style in childhood and adolescence. To a great degree, it is based on whether a person considers himself to be worthless, hopeless, valuable, or deserving.

An explanatory style also has these dimensions:

### Permanence or Persistence

According to Seligman, those who learn helplessness believe that bad events will *persist*. They therefore give up easily in the presence of negative circumstances because they believe the situation is likely to be permanent. They often have overgeneralized, distortional thinking, which we will discuss in Chapter 12.[24]

In the box-office hit *Annie*, the curly-topped, redheaded orphan croons her undying optimism: "The sun will come out tomorrow." Despite living in poverty and abandonment, Annie refuses to see her orphan status as permanent. She has not learned helplessness, and her character depicts the exact opposite: hopefulness.

### Pervasiveness

Seligman noted that individuals who make universal explanations for their failures believe that everything in life rides or falls on one experience. If they perceive themselves to have failed in one dimension of life, they see themselves as pervasively failing in *all* dimensions of life. They often have overgeneralized, "all-or-nothing" thinking. When confronted with an imperfection in one arena, they generalize it to reflect their entire identity. They strive to become perfectionists.

### Personalization

The helpless person personalizes external failures. He may blame himself for the consequences of an event over which he had no control—for example, assuming blame for financial loss because he personally failed to foresee the stock market crash in 1929. Some who manifest personalization blame individuals other than themselves; in the example of the stock market crash, they might blame a crooked accountant, an analyst, or a government official. The personalization can be internal or external. People who see external events as independent of personal blame have much higher self-esteem. Those who internalize and blame themselves when misfortune strikes tend to see themselves as worthless, hopeless, and helpless, all of which lead to low self-esteem.

## WHEN PERCEPTIONS ARE ASKEW

Those who learn helplessness give up easily and believe bad events will always persist. No cloud has a silver lining and nothing ever works out for the best. The future is destined to be marked by gray days and gloom.

If they burn the toast, they believe they can't do *anything* right. They are filled with self-blame and false guilt. Just like the dogs in Seligman's experiment, they lie down and whimper in the box rather than move away. They are psychologically stuck in their "stinking thinking."

When perceptions are askew, perceptions need to be changed. And they can be. The good news in all this is that whatever a person has acquired as a learned behavior he can also unlearn. Nobody needs to stay in a state of helplessness forever.

In the chapters that follow, you will learn how to replace "stinking thinking," or distortional thinking, with rational thinking—and in doing so you will be unlearning learned helplessness.

Most of our behavior is learned (yes, even depression) and can therefore be unlearned even if it is rooted in one's genes.

# 7

# THE DOWNWARD SPIRAL OF
# GUILT AND SHAME

Becky came into my office feeling, in her words, "really terrible." Becky was thirty-five years old at the time and the editor of a small magazine: a stressful, deadline-driven job. The particular company for which she worked was notoriously disorganized and the office tended to be chaotic. The owner had an extremely volatile disposition and at the slightest provocation, he sometimes flew off the handle and fired everyone in sight.

Years of emotional chaos had taken a toll on Becky's health. Many of her friends had lost their jobs or suffered the strain of emotional abuse in her workplace. Her boss repeatedly passed Becky over for raises that he gave only to women who were willing to flirt or offer sexual favors. As for Becky, the boss seemed only to have harsh, demeaning words of criticism.

Becky held great resentment and bitterness against this man. She blamed him for a host of ills in her life. Becky also felt ashamed. Overweight and plain in her appearance, she felt deeply humiliated by her boss every time he walked by—by his facial expressions, his words, his "rejection," his obvious feelings of disapproval. She actually sat in my examination room with a long sweater held up like a blanket to cover the front part of her fully clothed body. This, she admitted, was a longtime habit.

Becky's diagnosis was multiple sclerosis.

After speaking at length with Becky, I could not help but

conclude that her condition was linked in part to her emotionally turbulent life. Before she could get effective help for her physical complaints, she needed to be healed of her emotional wounds.

Becky was not only bitter about her employment situation, she felt great *shame,* a truly toxic emotion.

Shame, by formal definition, is a painful feeling of having lost the respect of others because of an improper behavior, sin, or label of incompetence. It arises from dishonor or disgrace stemming from something regrettable, unfortunate, or outrageous.

## CHRONIC GUILT AND SHAME CAN LEAD TO DEPRESSION

Our main reason to be concerned with guilt and shame in this book is this: these two states are commonly associated with major depression. Situational depression is usually the result of a major loss in a person's life—it may be a spouse, a child, a marriage, a job, a home, or some other major loss.

Guilt and shame are both rooted in what should *not* have occurred as much as in what *did* occur. Guilt is a state of having done something wrong or having committed an offense, legal or ethical. Guilt is a painful feeling of self-reproach for having done something that we recognize as being immoral, wrong, a crime, or sin. Shame generally arises from what *another* person has done, something that society widely recognizes as immoral, wrong, a crime, or sin—shame is the reflection onto the victim of an abuser's bad behavior.

GUILT AND SHAME ARE BOTH ROOTED IN WHAT SHOULD *NOT* HAVE OCCURRED AS MUCH AS IN WHAT *DID* OCCUR.

Guilt and shame evoke different responses in us. Shame tends to create feelings of deep sorrow and sadness, as well as a lack of self-worth. Guilt produces a certain amount of anger because we feel trapped at being caught or at having fallen victim to our own weaknesses. In both emotions, however, a feeling of being worthless, hopeless, or helpless may result. These feelings, in turn, can lead to depression, anger, anxiety, and an array of other toxic emotions that stimulate a stress response.

Many people link shame to painful memories of past rejection, which produce feelings of helplessless and hopelessless, or of extremely low self-value. These feelings result in depression in some, but in others, they may lead to anger, resentment, or rage.

Both guilt and shame create an endless circle of negative thinking. These emotions *never* lead to emotional freedom, strength, or health—either emotionally or physically.

## THE GREAT WEIGHT OF GUILT AND SHAME

People who feel guilt and shame often walk with stooped shoulders, their heads hanging. They convey the appearance that they want to hide, as Becky indicated with her sweater. It's an instinctual expression among us human beings to cower or seek to hide if we find ourselves in a situation that might cause us to be deeply embarrassed, guilty, or ashamed. It's not uncommon, for example, to see those arrested attempt to hide their faces or to turn away when the glare of public scrutiny—or the television camera of the nightly news team—lands on them.

Adam and Eve felt great shame in the Garden of Eden after they had disobeyed God. They attempted to hide from Him. They felt self-conscious, naked, exposed. That's what shame does to us. It leaves us feeling unworthy of approval, self-conscious, and as if our lack of value has been exposed. Shame makes us feel as if every person we encounter knows all about us, is scrutinizing us, and is critical of us—even if we admit with our rational minds that the vast majority of people we encounter don't know us or don't care about us.

Where do we learn shame?

Sadly, many people learn shame as children. And even more sadly, they learn it from their parents, who ridicule or humiliate them in front of their siblings or peers. A teacher, coach, or other authority figure, or even a school bully, can humiliate and shame children.

Sexual and physical abuse also may cause children to grow up feeling shame. Learning disabilities, such as dyslexia or attention deficit disorder, may cause children to be tagged as stupid, slow, dumb, or unable to learn. This is humiliating to youngsters—it may lead to long-standing feelings of shame.

Unfortunately, many children who bear the burden of shame carry their misery into adulthood. Adults who have deeply internalized shame often fear intimacy and bring commitment problems into marriage relationships. They struggle to maintain a marriage, sometimes drifting from marriage to marriage and breakup to breakup, never quite able to see their own self-sabotaging behavior as associated with the shame they carry like a giant, invisible weight deep within.

Adults who feel shame can end up enduring multiple affairs and divorces, a seemingly endless string of jobs, and can seem to sabotage close relationships. Their shame sends them wandering in something of a personal relationships wilderness. The repeated failures, of course, only add to the feelings of worthlessness, failure, and grief. Deep down, the shamed person feels he is genuinely unlovable and unworthy of anyone's care.

Deep depression often lies at the end of this emotional road. Shame may also lead to drug abuse, alcoholism, eating disorders, and out-of-control gambling, as well as other compulsive behaviors.

## TRUE OR FALSE GUILT?

Countless millions of people in our nation suffer tremendous guilt over past lifestyle choices or abuses such as affairs, abortions, sexual molestation, rape, and many other circumstances.

One woman who was riddled with guilt came to me a few years ago suffering from chronic fatigue and severe fibromyalgia. During Jane's exam, I learned that she had been through a divorce about two years prior to the onset of these conditions.

Right before her divorce, Jane discovered that her husband was having an affair with their neighbor, who also happened to be Jane's best friend. She found out about the affair in a most unusual way. Her best friend's husband learned about the affair first, and he came to Jane's house looking for her husband. When he found him, he gave Jane's husband such a severe beating that the man ended up in the intensive-care unit of a nearby hospital for a couple of weeks.

Jane, the dutiful wife, visited the hospital daily to take care of her husband, never fully grasping just why her neighbor attacked her husband. After doing this for two weeks, she went to the hospital to find her husband had been released. She asked at the nurses' station where her husband had gone, and the nurses informed her that his girlfriend had come to pick him up. Jane quickly began to put the pieces together, and when she did, she felt completely humiliated and ashamed.

Rather than label her husband a low-life scoundrel, Jane told me that she felt guilty. She felt that if she had been a trimmer, more attractive wife, her husband wouldn't have left her for her trimmer, more attractive friend.

I explained to Jane the difference between true guilt and false guilt. True guilt comes when we have done something we know is wrong, and we feel remorse for having done it (or at the minimum, for having been caught doing it). False guilt arises when we have done nothing wrong but we have been unwitting partners in someone else's sin, crime, or wrongdoing. False guilt is taking on one's self the guilt that rightfully belongs to another person. This is called "personalization," and is one of the ten types of negative life beliefs, or cognitive distortion, we will discuss in Chapter 12.

With true guilt, we need to forgive the person who wronged us, ask God for forgiveness, and then forgive ourselves for any part we may have played. With false guilt, we need to recognize that we have not done anything wrong, ask God to help us walk freely from the person who sinned, and forgive the person who hurt us so we might truly be unburdened in our emotions.

Jane chose to recognize her false guilt, forgive her husband and best friend, and become emotionally well. The process didn't happen overnight. It rarely does. The forgiving and releasing were a process that took about three months. But when that process was completed, Jane was amazed to find that both her fibromyalgia and chronic fatigue were gone.

## BRAIN VERSUS HEART

Like all toxic, damaging emotions, depression that comes from guilt or shame is primarily a matter of the heart. Most of us, however, do not listen to our hearts. We hear only our brains.

The brain is the taskmaster of the body—it never shuts up. It is designed to be on some level of alert at all times. Even as a person dreams, the brain attempts to sort out perceptions and emotions and make sense of life so the person can respond diligently.

The brain is protective and territorial. Paul Pearsall has written:

> The brain is not easily distracted from its lethal alliance with the body. It compulsively sticks to its task of trying to win the "human race." Author Thomas Moore writes of the Latin word "vocatio"—meaning to briefly pause from the pressures of daily living to wonder at being alive. Because the brain is primarily programmed to seek success and not the connection the heart craves, it barely tolerates such vacations.[1]

Pearsall contends that the brain is type A, while the heart reflects type B behavior. In other words, the brain is always in a hurry and uncomfortable with just being somewhere. Type A behavior—which is being critical, judgmental, harsh, cynical, blaming, controlling, and unforgiving—is the behavior dramatically linked to disease.

THE BRAIN IS TYPE A, WHILE THE HEART REFLECTS
TYPE B BEHAVIOR.

The type B "heart" behavior, in contrast, is gentle, relaxed, and searching for long-lasting relationships and intimacy. While the brain seems to "want to have a blast," in Pearsall's terms, the heart needs to "have a bond."

The brain believes in "I, me, mine," according to Pearsall. It is a natural pessimist. Psychologist Mihaly Csikszentmihalyi contends that the brain is biased toward pessimism because our ancestors were forced to remain ready to defend themselves against hostile predators.[2]

When the brain remains in the driver's seat, the heart—the soul, the seat of emotions—can be abused, wounded, exploited, and end up filled with hurt and pain. A heart that is filled with pain is a heart that is stressed, and often depressed.

Pearsall has also written:

Once the brain has abused the heart with its deadly, cynical code of self-preservation above all else, and driven the heart beyond its physiological limits, it can burn out its own life-support system. The heart is the most powerful muscle in the human body, but even it can be strained and torn by the pressures applied by a stressed and stressful brain.

When we neglect what our heart is trying to say to us and listen only to our brain we suffer the dangerous consequences of the "neglected heart syndrome" and health effects of abuse, deprivation, and exploitation of the sensitive side of who you are. Living in an increasingly heartless world only further assaults the heart. Yet, tuning in to our own hearts we could begin to experience the child within us, that most sensitive inner self that has the ability to teach us the joy of being alive.[3]

## LISTENING TO YOUR HEART

How can we learn to listen to our own hearts?

Many physicians I know ask their patients, "How do you feel?"

This is also the basic unverbalized question many of us confront every morning: "How do I feel today?" To become aware of your own emotional state, however, you must ask yourself, "How do I make others feel?"

If you are truly objective and honest with yourself, and you conclude that you seem to make others feel driven, controlled, angry, or hurt, there's a strong likelihood that you are brain-driven and that you are steamrolling over your own heart as well as over the heart of anyone who stands in your path.

I believe it is especially important for people to own up to feelings of guilt or shame in their own hearts. This is a vital key to unlocking health and wholeness.

The Bible says, "The heart knows its own bitterness, And a stranger does not share its joy" (Prov. 14:10). The hurts, pains, disappointments, delayed hopes, and broken dreams of your life are all hidden in the deep chambers of your heart.

A great deal of healing from depression can come as a person gains an understanding of the assault that the brain has made against the heart. A person first must understand that the human heart really *does* understand the depth of its own suffering. Ultimately, you don't need another person to tell you how you feel—you *know* how you feel. You know all of the emotions that lie deep within. You may not readily know how to access those emotions, but they are there nonetheless. The goal we face is to learn to recognize what the heart is trying to say. To understand the depth of our own wounds, we each must learn the language of our own heart.

> TO UNDERSTAND THE DEPTH OF OUR OWN WOUNDS, WE
> EACH MUST LEARN THE LANGUAGE OF OUR OWN HEART.

A cancer survivor once explained how his heart "spoke" to him in very soft messages. He believed he might have spared himself a great deal of physical agony had he learned to listen to his heart sooner. He said:

I learned through my cancer that when the heart speaks, it does so much as a shy child tries to get her busy mother's attention by repeatedly tugging on her skirt. Like a baby's frustrated cry as it tries to express its needs without words, my heart sobbed in a primal language that can be understood only when we allow our heart to enter into the constant dialogue between our brain and its body . . . our heart has a very delicate way in which it tries to get our attention, and to hear, we must focus on our chest and not our head.[4]

When a newborn infant smiles at you for the first time, when the one you love sends you a sentimental Valentine's Day card, when your teenage son puts his arm around you and says, "I love you," where do you feel touched?

In the heart!

Often we touch our hands to our hearts when we feel especially loved, complimented, accepted, or overwhelmed at the generosity another person has shown. Conversely, when we feel wounded, we also feel that wound in our hearts.

## THE GOOD NEWS

The good news is that broken hearts can be mended. We can learn to cherish, nourish, and protect this most precious and sensitive part of our being.

Linda, whose story I shared with you in the previous chapter on depression, was able to overcome her fibromyalgia, lose weight, and break free from the terrible bondage of depression and guilt. She did so by recognizing first and foremost that she *could* change the damaging thought processes that had led to her wounding and depression. She learned to get in touch with her own heart and to isolate the deep feelings that she had long repressed. She also learned to have hope—she learned to believe in the ever-present possibility of love, appreciation, joy, peace, and human dignity in every person's heart.

What happened in her heart and in her whole being . . . can happen to you.

The good news for those suffering from guilt or shame is this: Jesus died on the cross to remove the stain of guilt and shame from our lives. I encourage you to receive His merciful, free, and generous gift of forgiveness and freedom from these toxic emotions. Then forgive yourself and move forward in your life!

# 8

# THE EMOTIONAL POISON OF FEAR

Mark almost didn't get the opportunity to tell me his story. He had come to see me for an exercise and dietary prescription in the wake of coronary-artery bypass surgery. As we talked, I told Mark that I had been spending my evening hours in recent months doing more extensive research into the mind-body connection. He expressed interest in the idea that damaging emotions and deadly diseases are often linked.

"Give me an example of a toxic emotion," Mark said.

"Sure," I replied. "How about fear?"

Mark stared back at me with a wide-eyed expression. "Are you reading my mind?" he asked.

"No," I said. "Why?"

"Because I think there's a direct link between fear and the heart attack that revealed my need for bypass surgery."

Mark went on to relate his story. He told me that all his life people had called him a "scaredy-cat"—not only his childhood peers but also his father, grandfather, uncle, and other adults. He had been left alone quite a bit as a child. His father and mother had been ministers, and it seems they often were called away to parishioners' homes in the middle of the night. Mark, as the eldest child, was left in charge during those emergency late-night calls. He felt a tremendous responsibility and was scared most of the time that something dreadful would happen in their absence, or even worse, that something dreadful would happen to his parents and they might not return.

On top of this, Mark's parents were ministers in a very strict denomination. Mark grew up afraid that something awful would happen to him because he was certain he had sinned in ways that he didn't know about, and therefore, he was living with unconfessed and unforgiven sin. He feared what God might do to him as a sinner.

"On top of all that," Mark concluded, "my grandpa, dad, and two uncles were real outdoorsmen. They liked to fish and hunt and they took me along. I didn't particularly like the idea of sleeping in a tent in the outdoors, which had lots of animal sounds that were unfamiliar to me. That's really when the label of 'scaredy-cat' took hold."

"What do you think this has to do with your heart attack?" I asked.

"Well, the night that I had the attack I heard steps on the wooden deck outside our master bedroom door. I awoke from a deep sleep hearing this noise, which sounded to me like somebody with heavy boots trying to walk quietly on the deck. I'd like to tell you that I jumped up and scared what I perceived to be our attacker away, but I didn't. I felt paralyzed, glued flat to the bed. I broke out in a cold sweat. The more I tried to move, the less I was able to move and the more I second-guessed what would happen if I did. My heart started racing and before I knew it, I was having serious chest pain. I guess I must have called my wife's name because she awoke, jumped up, and called 911 before I could protest. I'm glad she did."

Then Mark got very quiet. "Please don't tell her what I just told you. I never told her about the footsteps I heard on the deck. I don't want to alarm her."

"Did you ever find any evidence of a burglar in the neighborhood?" I asked.

"No," Mark said. "What I did discover is that the people next door had acquired a huge dog the day before this happened. When I think back on it now, that dog may very well have jumped their fence and explored our deck. To have a heart attack over a curious dog would really be bizarre."

Mark's experience was not uncommon. Many people live with

enormous fear just below the surface of their lives—a fear that can turn deadly.

"But," you may say, "Mark's fear was unfounded."

That doesn't matter. Phantom fears—those that aren't rooted in reality—are just as real to the body as genuine danger. We all know the experience of thinking that a hose in the yard might be a snake, or that a clump of lint might be a large spider. One woman told me about seeing a fake snake that the previous owners of her home had apparently put in a flowerbed to scare away flower-eating critters. She said, "I nearly fainted dead away when I saw that thing. Fortunately, I went to get a shovel to decapitate it and when I returned, I found the snake hadn't moved. It was in the same position I had left it. I don't think my heart quit beating hard for about ten minutes."

Since the terrorist attacks on our nation in September 2001, fear and anxiety seem to have hit an all-time high in the United States. Many people have a foreboding sense of dread that a 9/11 incident just may happen again. Fear of the unknown is just as forceful as fear of the well known. And all types of fear can be deadly.

## FEAR'S ASSOCIATION WITH DISEASE

Fear has been associated with a wide variety of diseases, including cardiovascular diseases and hypertension; digestive-tract diseases such as colitis, Crohn's disease, irritable bowel syndrome, and ulcers; headaches; and skin disorders such as psoriasis, eczema, and stress acne. Fear can cause a decreased immune response, which may lead to frequent infections or the development of deadly disease. Fear can precede a heart attack, as in Mark's case, or even death.

Fear is a powerful emotion that produces a very potent pschological response. History holds countless stories of individuals whose fear reached such an overwhelming level that they fell over dead.

One of the classic examples of the toxic power of fear appears in the Bible. The story involves a man named Nabal, whose name means "fool" (see 1 Sam. 25). The meaning of this man's name may be a first indicator to his anger management problems—doesn't overreacting and boiling rage make fools of us at times?

Nabal was a very wealthy man, with three thousand sheep and one thousand goats, which by anyone's standards is a lot of livestock. Livestock in the desert economy of Bible times was better than gold.

Livestock owners such as Nabal relied heavily upon vigilantes to protect their herds and flocks. Fortunately for Nabal, David provided just such a service to him.

At that time, David had been anointed to be the next king of Israel, but he had not yet assumed the throne. God had rejected the current king, Saul, but he was still in power. King Saul was less than happy about this state of affairs and in his great jealousy of David, he sought to kill him. David was running for his life. A ragtag group of men had associated with David so that he had several hundred men and their families surrounding him in the wilderness areas where he hid out from King Saul and his men. Part of the way David supported this group of men was by receiving monetary "reward" and payment in food from the people whose livestock they helped secure.

During the sheep-shearing season, when the livestock was gathered from wilderness grazing areas, David sent some of his men to Nabal to request the payment that was normally due for the services they had provided through the year. This was a time when livestock owners were usually very generous. Nabal, however, refused the men's request, pretending to be completely unaware of David, his men, and their activities.

When David heard of Nabal's response—which was an open affront as well as a serious financial loss—he was furious. He also knew that word of Nabal's refusal was likely to spread, which meant that other livestock owners might follow his example. This was something David could not afford. The future king commanded his men to take up their swords. David was determined to get what was rightfully owed to him and his men, even if it took armed conflict.

When Nabal's wife, Abigail, learned of her husband's foolish response, she acted quickly to save her household. She packed several donkeys with a generous gift of two hundred loaves of bread, two skins of wine, five sheep already slaughtered and dressed, five bushels of roasted grain, a hundred clusters of raisins, and two hundred cakes of figs. Abigail didn't tell Nabal what she was doing. Instead she quickly and quietly ordered her servants to take the food to David, and then she followed to plead the case for her household before David himself.

When Abigail reached David, she fell at his feet and begged forgiveness for her husband's foolish, greedy, and mean-spirited actions. She encouraged David to lay aside his anger, to accept the gift she had arranged, and to grant her request for peace between David and her household. David agreed.

Abigail returned home to find Nabal hosting a feast fit for a king. The Bible tells us "Nabal's heart was merry within him, for he was very drunk" (1 Sam. 25:36). Abigail knew upon returning home that her husband wasn't capable of rationally hearing and responding to what she had done, so she waited until the next day to tell him. When she did tell him how close he had come to being killed, along with all of his servants, "his heart died within him, and he became like a stone" (v. 37). In other words, he suffered a severe heart attack that left him in a comatose state. Ten days later, he died.

Jesus warned that circumstances can and will arise in this world that result in "men's hearts failing them from fear" (Luke 21:26).

World events and personal crises are two sources of deathly fear. Voodoo may be another. People in some third world nations still practice voodoo as a religion. A number of researchers have studied death in voodoo rituals. Cardiologist Dr. Regis DeSilva and fellow researcher Wade Davis believe voodoo deaths are actually cases of sudden death resulting from fear.[1] Excessive stimulation of the stress response, called "sympathetic stimulation," may cause the heart to go into fibrillation, such as ventricular fibrillation or ventricular tachycardia, either of which is capable of causing sudden death. In other words, the people who die in voodoo rituals are literally scared to death. The great fear they experience stimulates the sympathetic nervous system to such a degree that the heart actually goes into extremely rapid and unstoppable beating (ventricular fibrillation), which in turn causes sudden death.

THE PEOPLE WHO DIE IN VOODOO RITUALS ARE
LITERALLY SCARED TO DEATH.

## WHAT HAPPENS WHEN YOU ARE AFRAID?

The amygdala is the particular portion of the brain that controls fear and anxiety. It is located deep within the brain, not far from the hippocampus, the area of the brain that controls memory and helps the brain learn and retain information.

As is the case with all intense, toxic emotions, a chemical response occurs in the brain when a person experiences severe fear. This chemical activity excites these vital brain centers in particular.

Fear and anxiety seem to occur on the same general spectrum. Fear is a concentrated, short-term bout of anxiety. It's the acute, immediate "anxious" response.

Most people recover quickly after they've experienced fear. In addition, the cause of fear is generally easy to recognize: the noise in the night, the person who cut in front of you in rapidly flowing traffic, the loud bang that seemed too close for comfort.

Some fears occur repeatedly in the same environment; in other words, certain experiences or circumstances always seem to trigger fear in a person. In these cases, the fear is called a *phobia*. Phobias are irrational—there's usually no obvious or known reason for why a person reacts with extreme fear. Some have an unrealistic fear of heights. Now, most people have a healthy fear of heights; they aren't likely to walk right up to the edge of a sheer-faced cliff and lean over to look at the bottom of the gorge several hundred feet below. But an extreme fear of or phobia about heights can keep a person from taking an exterior-wall glass elevator or going too close to the window of an office that is on the third floor.

I recently heard about a woman who has a great fear of tigers. She won't go near the "big cat" area of a zoo, won't see a motion picture that features tigers, and whenever possible she avoids even looking at photographs of tigers that may be a part of an advertisement or a magazine article. There's no rationality to her fear. It exists nonetheless.

Part of the definition of a phobia is that it is a crippling fear. It keeps a person from moving about normally in society. For example, the person with a phobia about heights may not be able to drive across a high bridge without panicking. That's going to curtail such a person's mobility. Those who suffer from agoraphobia—fear of the marketplace—find it nearly impossible to go shopping in a supermarket or walk through an airport. They break out in a cold sweat anytime they find themselves in an area where many other people may be milling about. Some people have phobias about specific animals or insects, such as snakes, rats, or spiders.

When a person has a sudden attack of fear, the body responds with an intense and acute stress response: adrenaline flows into the bloodstream and immediately signals the body to go on its highest level of alert to fight or flee.

In most cases, even in cases of intense fear and phobia, the stress response will shut down as soon as the circumstance that caused the fear changes. In others, however, the stress response does not shut down. Stress hormones continue to pour into the body. In those cases, the cardiovascular or immune system can suffer damage.

The release of stress hormones during a phobic or other type of fear attack can cause palpitations or rapid heartbeat, elevated blood pressure, and other uncomfortable cardiovascular symptoms.

## ANXIETY, OVERCARE, AND FEAR

Is it possible to care too much? Yes. Overcare describes a condition in which a person overidentifies with or becomes overattached to what he cares about. It's at that point that care becomes overcare.

The person who is the recipient of overcare activity is under a great deal of stress. So is the person who does the overcaring!

When care turns to overcare, its recipient begins to feel worried, anxious, guilty, threatened, fearful, and even angry. Overcare actually makes a person feel as if he's just eaten five pounds of chocolate. He feels smothered and seeks to escape.

Doc Childre has written: "Most of the time when people get anxious, angry, over-reactive, or manipulative, they are caring about something, but in a draining and unusually ineffective way . . . The mind turns our genuinely caring intention into a mental and emotional drain."[2]

Our grandparents' generation tended to calm themselves by saying, "Live and let live." In our generation, however, we tend to do just the opposite. Like the tiny child who loved her pet chick so much that she squeezed it to death, we hold everything too tightly.

One of my patients seemed to be a professional when it came to overcare. Brandy was a pretty woman: tall, thin, with long, black curly hair and a personality that lit up whatever room she entered. Everyone loved to be around Brandy. She could turn even the most mundane event into a party. So why did Brandy, who was nearly fifty years old when I met her, have no prospects for marriage and a long list of past heartbreaks and painful relationships?

The main reason was her overcaring behavior. She had so much passion and zest for life, and she wanted a relationship so desperately, that when she finally landed a guy, she sent him running for the nearest exit with her overcare. She began every relationship with a premature assault of calls, gifts, letters, notes, and other tokens of her affection. She took it upon herself to meet all his relatives, call all his friends, and make connections with all of his connections. If his head wasn't already spinning, she would change anything about herself that she thought he didn't like. Once while dating a particular man who liked country music, she began to wear denim and cowboy boots and even purchased a horse! She had never sat on a saddle in her life, and she didn't really enjoy "things Western," but she felt she needed to change because she "cared."

The men in Brandy's life experienced tremendous anxiety in the wake of her overcare and they all backed off as quickly as possible. Brandy was left with the exact opposite of what she truly desired. As a consequence of her overcare she was miserable.

In many ways, we have become a society infected with many people who overcare.

How does overcare relate to fear? It is rooted in a fear of some type of loss—perhaps loss of control, of one's identity, of not achieving what a person truly feels he *needs* in order to live.

Brandy had a fear that if she didn't find a guy to marry, she would not have the life she deeply desired.

Always at the root of overcare is a long-term and abiding fear of abandonment, rejection, and loss. When we respond to these fear-generating emotions in our lives, we set ourselves up for a pattern of behavior that not only makes us psychologically unhealthy but can make us physically unhealthy.

## THE ANTIDOTE FOR FEAR AND WORRY

When you sense your heart filling with fear or your mind crowding with thoughts of irreversible loss, take a minute to ask yourself, "What *right now* seems to be fueling this fear?" As best you can, pinpoint the cause of your stress and the source of the fear. And then seek to deal with those issues.

Are you overcaring? Are you hanging on to or pursuing things that aren't necessary, or perhaps aren't part of God's plan for your life? Are you caring to the point of stressing yourself or the person you care about?

Faith is the ultimate cure for fear. Faith is believing that God is in charge of all things and that we can rely on Him to do what is eternally best for each of us. I encourage you strongly: Choose to believe that God is at work in your life and in the lives of those around you. Choose to believe that God is in control of all situations and all circumstances. Faith is always a *choice*—one I encourage you to make daily!

FAITH IS THE ULTIMATE CURE FOR FEAR. FAITH IS
BELIEVING THAT GOD IS IN CHARGE OF ALL THINGS
AND THAT WE CAN RELY ON HIM TO DO WHAT IS
ETERNALLY BEST FOR EACH OF US.

Jesus taught, "Let not your heart be troubled; you believe in God, believe also in Me" (John 14:1). Repeatedly in the Scriptures, Jesus or an angel of the Lord spoke to people with these words: "Fear not!" When it comes to fear, may those words from God ring in our hearts always, in all situations and circumstances, in all relationships, in all our dreams and hopes and desires.

# 9

# WHEN WORRY TURNS DEADLY

It was almost too easy. Wanda came into my office and openly and freely admitted in one of her first statements to me, "I'm a worrier. People have been calling me a 'worrywart' all my life." From that moment on, it was difficult to think of Wanda in any terms other than "Wanda the worrywart."

Wanda recognized that worry, a deep feeling of ongoing anxiety, was likely linked to the host of ailments she experienced. Treatment of Wanda's worry became as much our concern as treatment of her physical symptoms.

As a whole, we are a nation of worriers. The Mitchum Report on Stress in the 1990s revealed that work, money, and family are constant sources of stress for most people in the United States. More than half of all adult Americans stated in this report that they worry most about work or money.[1]

Anxiety disorders are the most common mental illness in the United States. About nineteen million Americans are afflicted. A *Time*/CNN poll taken eight months after the 9/11 attack on our nation revealed that at that time nearly two-thirds of all Americans thought about the terrorist attacks at least "a few times a week."[1]

As is the case with fear, anxiety has been associated with a host of deadly conditions including cardiovascular diseases, hypertension, colitis and Crohn's disease, irritable bowel syndrome, ulcers, headaches, skin disorders such as psoriasis, eczema, and stress acne, and a decreased immune response, which can open up a person to even more serious illness.

Many people, however—unlike Wanda—don't see any harm in their tendency to worry. Let me ask you today:

Do you lie awake worrying about whether you are about to lose your job? Do you feel a knot in the pit of your stomach when you think about the stock market or your retirement plan?

Do you fret all morning when your boss comes into work in a bad mood?

Do you feel as if you go to bed drained of all hope and energy after watching several hours of prime-time news and programs that seem to be about nothing but violence, terror, or war?

Do you *know* you are sacrificing your health for the sake of worrying about the next step in your career?

## WHAT IS AN ANXIETY DISORDER?

Anxiety is the unpleasant sense of apprehension that accompanies physical symptoms such as sweaty palms, shallow breathing, rapid heart rate, and general nervousness. Anxiety is more abiding than fear—it is a feeling that lingers long after an actual threat has passed.

Anxiety that is of less intensity is what we call "fretting" or "worry." Anxiety, however, can also be of high intensity. In those cases, an anxiety disorder may exist. In the medical world, we call this *pathologic anxiety.*

Anxiety disorders are fairly common. They include generalized anxiety disorders, post-traumatic stress disorders, panic disorders, obsessive-compulsive disorders, and phobias.

Some anxiety disorders are more dangerous to the physical body than others. The most threatening are those that create a release of stress hormones that doesn't shut down after a particular experience or event is over. Let's look at these in more detail.

*Generalized Anxiety Disorder*

Generalized anxiety disorder (GAD) is an anxiety state that is usually chronic. People with GAD feel anxiety about a wide variety of life circumstances, pretty much all the time. If they aren't fretting over the high cost of milk today they may be worrying about what *might* happen to skew their vacation plans or whether they forgot to check all the doors before leaving on an errand. For those with GAD, life always has *something* that warrants their concern. They usually can't imagine why others aren't more concerned, and they sometimes feel that it is up to them to be concerned since nobody else seems to be.

## Post-Traumatic Stress Disorder

Post-traumatic stress disorder (PTSD) usually occurs in the wake of a terrifying ordeal, such as rape, car-jacking, armed robbery, or any other major traumatic event. A number of Vietnam veterans suffered from PTSD. This form of anxiety disorder may also occur during a divorce or after the death of a loved one.

Those with PTSD can spend an entire day replaying mental and emotional tapes of the stressful event or series of events they have experienced. They may suffer from nightmares. They sometimes overreact when harmless events or inanimate objects trigger memories of their traumas.

One of my patients, whom I'll call Andrea, was robbed while she was working at a quick-stop store on the edge of town. A masked gunman entered the store just as she was closing up for the evening. He forced her to lie facedown on the floor while he held a gun to her head. After taking some money from the cash register, he fled.

Today, more than a year after the event, every time Andrea hears a door creak open, smells the aroma of the cleaning fluid that was used on the quick-stop store's floors, or drives by a quick-stop store, she becomes extremely anxious.

For some, the post-traumatic stress response occurs many years after the event. One man told me about experiencing such a PTSD incident while he was touring Israel several years ago. He heard the launch of a test rocket while he was in the far northern area of the Golan Heights and he immediately fell to the ground in a full-body, prone position. He could hardly get up—he was nearly frozen in that position for several minutes. Fortunately, he and his wife were with a tour guide on a private tour so he had little residual embarrassment associated with this attack. He was concerned, nonetheless, that he could still experience fear so intensely, since it had been thirty years since he was a soldier in Vietnam. He told me, "I couldn't believe how strongly I felt that automatic response to hit the deck. I thought all that was behind me." For some, PTSD never goes away completely.

## Panic Disorder

An amazing number of Americans—a whopping 2.4 million adults in the United States—are affected by panic disorders.[2] With a panic disorder, overwhelming feelings of terror or anxiety seize a person suddenly and without warning. A panic attack may happen while a person is driving her car on a busy interstate, or while he is in an auditorium filled with PTA parents. A brooding sense of impending doom often accompanies panicky feelings. The fact that a person doesn't know when and where a panic attack may occur just adds to his overall anxiety.

> AN AMAZING NUMBER OF AMERICANS—A WHOPPING
> 2.4 MILLION ADULTS IN THE UNITED STATES—
> ARE AFFECTED BY PANIC DISORDERS.

A panic attack triggers a typical stress response, shooting adrenaline into the sufferer's bloodstream. As is the case with sudden fear and other toxic emotions, this adrenaline rush causes the heart to beat faster and harder. It is not uncommon for a person with a panic disorder to have heart palpitations and even chest pains, to the point that he thinks he is having a heart attack. The person may also have sweaty palms and a dry mouth and experience nausea, abdominal pain, trembling, dizziness, or a choking sensation.

A man named Mike came to me with an extreme case of panic disorder. He had a panic attack at least once a week, and usually while he was driving. Suddenly he would feel chest pain, numbness down his left arm, palpitations of the heart, and shortness of breath. Thinking he was having a heart attack, he immediately drove himself to the nearest emergency room. Adding to his overall state of anxiety, of course, was the fact that Mike never knew when he really might be having a heart attack.

Mike had a fairly high monthly bill for emergency-room treatment until he finally received treatment for panic disorder.

During a panic attack, a person's blood pressure may skyrocket to an extremely high level. One of my patients had a blood pressure reading of 220/140 during a panic attack he experienced in my office. As soon as the attack was over, his blood pressure returned to 120/80. Such a dramatic stress response in the body, over time and repeated attacks, may cause a person to develop hypertension, cardiovascular disease, or stroke.

### Obsessive-Compulsive Disorder

Yet another type of anxiety disorder is the obsessive-compulsive disorder. With this, disturbing ideas or images flood the person's mind—this is the obsessive part of the disorder. The sufferer then creates routine, repetitive rituals to rid the mind of these images. One of the most famous characters in theatrical literature depicting an obsessive-compulsive disorder is Lady Macbeth in Shakespeare's *Macbeth*. Lady Macbeth saw the image of blood on her hands after she committed a murder. She washed her hands again and again to rid herself of the feelings of guilt associated with this mental image. Her hand-washing, of course, had no effect whatsoever—it was a meaningless and repetitious behavior because it did not absolve her of her guilt. Such a routine and repeated ritual is the compulsive part of an obsessive-compulsive disorder.

One of the most common obsessive-compulsive disorders involves anxiety about germs. People with this condition routinely and ritualistically wash their hands after touching any object at all—even a doorknob, pencil, or telephone. Others draw back rather than risk shaking hands with a person. Some people with this particular disorder wash their hands hundreds of times a day.

Many people who have this anxiety disorder realize that the rituals they are performing make little sense. Nevertheless, they are unable to stop.

I once witnessed an extreme example of this behavior in a patient named Eloise. This middle-aged woman washed her hands incessantly and worked tirelessly, day and night, to keep her house free of germs. She vacuumed and cleaned from sunup to sundown. Anyone who entered her house had to take off his shoes at the door. She followed her guests around with a spray bottle, disinfecting doorknobs and countertops they touched. You can imagine how stressful life was for those who visited Eloise. The fact is, Eloise's behavior was stressing her out. When she came to my office, she was nervous, fidgety, and exhausted from her endless cleaning routine. I was able to help her with medication and a referral for psychotherapy.

The disorders I've mentioned here—generalized anxiety disorder, post-traumatic stress disorder, panic disorder, and obsessive-compulsive disorder—all cause stimulation of the stress response. And that leads to elevated levels of adrenaline and cortisol.

## ANXIETY'S MORE EVERYDAY FORMS

### General Worry

About nineteen million Americans suffer from anxiety disorders, but far more suffer from mild anxiety that has not yet developed to the disorder state. Experiencing severe or continual anxiety isn't necessarily pathological—meaning that a person has an emotional or mental disturbance. In many of these people, worry has simply become a mental habit. They automatically tend to see events in their lives in terms of worst-case scenarios. If his teenager takes the car out in the evening, he spends the entire time the child is away worrying that he may be killed in an accident. If she plans a trip home to visit her grandchildren, she worries that a terrorist might be on her plane.

The worrier may lie awake at night going through a series of "what if" possibilities. As with any mental habit that becomes ingrained in the brain, this habit of general worry tends to get worse over time.

### Dread

Dread leads to distorted thinking, a state that can lead to lack of hope and despair. The greater the anxiety and dread, the greater the release of stress hormones.

### Worry About Things

Many people have anxiety that is not person-related, but rather thing-related. As a nation, we seem to be consumed with the concept of consuming! Instead of human beings, we're becoming "human doings." We collect things, store things, hold garage sales to rid ourselves of things, purchase space to store other things we rarely use, and spend countless hours shopping for things to replace, update, or add to the stuff we already own. Many people shower their stuff with overcare. They spend hours every week sorting, cleaning, and generally fiddling with their material possessions, especially perhaps those of the electronic variety that they are still figuring out how to work.

A woman told me just recently that she always knew when her college-age son was stressed out. She said, "He'd either go fishing, which was relaxing, or he'd spend hours that he could have spent studying in sorting all of his fishing lures and tackles." This young man was into overcare of his material stuff—in his case, this concern about things was a reflection of stress, not a cause of stress.

The Bible has strong words for those who overcare about money and possessions:

"He who trusts in his riches will fall, But the righteous will flourish like foliage" (Prov. 11:28).

Jesus taught, "Seek first the kingdom of God and His righteousness, and all these things shall be added to you" (Matt. 6:33). Seeking the kingdom of God includes being genuinely grateful for the things the Lord has given to you, and being determined to spend quality time alone with God in prayer and quiet reflection on

His Word. Seeking first the kingdom is in contrast with striving to acquire wealth, status, or possessions. It is also in sharp contrast with striving to control people or situations.

## THE LINK BETWEEN ANXIETY AND DISEASE

A significant number of physical complaints and serious diseases have been linked to anxiety, including cardiovascular disease, ulcers, irritable bowel syndrome, and illnesses related to decreased immune function. One of the foremost ailments is the headache—both the tension headache and the migraine.

Tension causes about 90 percent of all headaches.[3] You are a rare individual if you've never suffered one. Tension headaches usually occur during a stressful season at work, a high-tension time in a relationship, or a difficult financial period. I can only guess how many people stay up late doing their taxes on April 15 only to lie awake afterward with a major tension headache.

Anxiety creates stress that particularly strikes the muscles in the upper back and neck. As these muscles tighten and become over-fatigued, they spasm and create headaches.

Migraine headaches, in contrast, generally are vascular in origin. Their cause is the dilation of blood vessels in the head. The same stress that causes a tension headache may trigger the thundering pain of a migraine, but the body internalizes the stress in the blood vessels rather than the muscles.

If you routinely experience headaches, your body is trying to tell you that something is wrong and you need to take action. Many times what is wrong is too much stress—you may be too anxious or too worried. Simple relaxation techniques and refocusing thoughts work well in many people to abort a headache before it can become full-blown.

### Anxiety and Cardiovascular Diseases

An anxiety disorder—whether post-traumatic stress disorder, obsessive-compulsive disorder, or generalized anxiety disorder—

turns on a stress response that causes epinephrine to flood the body. Blood pressure is very vulnerable to epinephrine. Too much epinephrine, and blood pressure can skyrocket. When this happens, the smooth endothelial lining of the arteries can develop very tiny nicks and tears. This damage frequently occurs at the points where the arteries branch out, especially in the coronary and carotid arteries.

If the person's blood is loaded with fatty deposits that make platelets stickier and more susceptible to forming clumps, the environment is ripe for the formation of cardiovascular disease and plaque buildup.

Several research studies have shown anxiety disorders leading to greater risk of carotid artery disease. In one study covering a four-year time span, men who experienced anxiety for an extended period of time showed a higher increase of plaque in the carotid arteries than men who did not have sustained anxiety.[4]

Research studies have documented a link between coronary artery disease and panic disorders, as well as between cardiovascular disease and worry. One study showed that anxiety and sudden death appear to be connected. In this study, researchers concluded that ventricular arrhythmias (a dangerous rhythm of the heart) may have been the mechanism for sudden death among individuals with anxiety disorders, as opposed to a heart attack that generally involves blood clotting.[5]

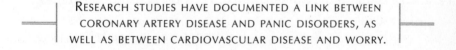

RESEARCH STUDIES HAVE DOCUMENTED A LINK BETWEEN CORONARY ARTERY DISEASE AND PANIC DISORDERS, AS WELL AS BETWEEN CARDIOVASCULAR DISEASE AND WORRY.

### Anxiety and Ulcers

For many centuries Chinese acupuncturists have believed that the stomach and spleen are connected to the emotion of anxiety. They may well be right. We are learning more about the mind-body connection all the time, and when it comes to ulcers, this theory seems to have bearing on the activity of a particular bacteria.

Medical researchers today believe that up to 95 percent of patients with duodenal ulcers and 80 percent of patients with gastric ulcers are infected with heliobacter pylori (H-pylori).[6] How can anxiety and a bacteria be related?

First, stress significantly slows down the release of digestive juices, including hydrochloric acid and digestive enzymes. The body shunts blood flow away from the digestive tract and redirects it to the muscles to prepare them for a fight-or-flight response.

Another way of saying this is that stress turns on the sympathetic nervous system and turns off the parasympathetic nervous system. It is the parasympathetic nervous system that aids digestion—it is the nervous system that operates when a person is calm and relaxed. This is one reason it is important to be relaxed and comfortable when you eat.

When the stomach and digestive tract have a decrease in digestive juices, the microscopic bacteria called H-pylori can thrive.

Most peoplle who have this bacteria do not exhibit symptoms. But when the mucosal lining of the stomach or small intestine gets damaged by aspirin, ibuprofin, and other anti-inflammatory medications, or from alcohol or infection, these bacteria can do great damage in that area. An ulcer forms when there's a break or hole in the mucosal surface that is greater than five millimeters in size.

Once damage or irritation occurs, H-pylori colonization can produce even more inflammation. Most peptic ulcers (both gastric in the stomach and duodenal in the first part of the small intestines) are the result of the combination of H-pylori and anti-inflammatory medication.

How does this relate to anxiety? We know that the United States has a far higher incidence of ulcers in proportion to its population than third world nations do.[7] The prevailing theory is that Americans suffer more stress and have more anxiety disorders—which results in symptoms such as pain and soreness from the stress hormones released into the body. To compensate for the pain and soreness, we take more anti-inflammatory medications.

*Anxiety and Irritable Bowel Syndrome*

Another common disorder linked to anxiety is irritable bowel syndrome (IBS), which is the most common gastrointestinal disorder in the United States. IBS affects approximately one out of every five Americans. Nearly 50 percent of office visits to gastroenterologists are IBS related.[8]

The symptoms of this syndrome include abdominal pain and cramping, abdominal bloating or swelling, constipation and diarrhea, mucus in the stool, and an unnatural, extreme urgency to have a bowel movement.

When the body's stress response kicks into high gear, this causes the large intestines to move spontaneously, which generally results in diarrhea. The colon increases contractions, or peristalsis, to dump out whatever is in it to decrease the "load" a person has to carry if he is put into fight-or-flight mode.

At the same time the brain signals the large intestines to empty, it sends the opposite signal to the small intestines. Motility, or spontaneous movement, decreases. At times the stress reaction can cause too much decrease in the small intestines without significantly increasing the activity of the large intestines. This results in constipation. It is not uncommon for those with irritable bowel syndrome to experience alternating bouts of diarrhea and constipation.

*Anxiety and Other Digestive-Tract Diseases*

Stress can aggravate other diseases of the stomach, intestines, and bowels, such as ulcerative colitis and Crohn's disease. These diseases very often tend to go into remission when a person brings his stress levels under control.

*Anxiety and Decreased Immune Response*

Chronic anxiety produces stress, and as is true for all stress-producing emotions, the result is a depressed immune response. This, in turn, results in greater susceptibility to infections, including the common cold.[9]

## ANXIETY'S MOST SEVERE RESULT

While most anxiety attacks do *not* lead to death, extreme anxiety can cause death. The Bible gives us a dramatic story related to a severe anxiety attack. The story involves a husband and wife named Ananias and Sapphira (see Acts 5).

This couple had made a display of a very generous offering before all of their friends at the time when the Christian church was just beginning in Jerusalem. The presence and miracle-working power of God appeared in dramatic ways in this first group of believers in Jesus. While the believers themselves, including Ananias and Sapphira, were deeply committed to accepting and following Jesus as Messiah, many of their Jewish family members were not. The new believers were ostracized from the society at large. In order to live, they pooled their resources. Many sold their lands and other possessions in order to share with those who had nothing and were in danger of starving. Ananias and Sapphira had announced that they would be among those who were selling all for the sake of the new church.

There was only one problem: they didn't turn everything over to the church. They kept back part of the money they received for the property they sold. They *pretended* to give the total sum as an act of great faith and generosity, when in truth they were lying to their fellow believers. The way the story appears in the Bible, Ananias and Sapphira seemed to want the social prestige and recognition that came with the making of a wholehearted gift. Their gift was not an act of faith, nor was it a gift made with the pure motives of love and goodwill.

By divine insight, the apostle Peter recognized that Ananias had been deceitful. He said to him as he laid the gift of money at Peter's feet, "Why has Satan filled your heart to lie to the Holy Spirit and keep back part of the price of the land for yourself? While it remained, was it not your own? And after it was sold, was it not in your own control? Why have you conceived this thing in your heart? You have not lied to men but to God." When Ananias heard these words, he "fell down and breathed his last" (Acts 5:3–5).

Three hours later when Sapphira showed up, not knowing what had happened, Peter confronted her and asked, "Tell me whether you sold the land for so much?" She said, "Yes, for so much." Peter realized she had been in on the deceit and told her what had happened to Ananias. The Bible tells us, "Then immediately she fell down at his feet and breathed her last" (Acts 5:8, 10).

Ananias and Sapphira both experienced sudden death, very possibly from an arrhythmia or heart attacks brought on by panic attacks. Both of these individuals found themselves in a situation in which they felt suddenly exposed, suddenly subjected to the ridicule of those they thought they were going to impress, suddenly confronted with the reality that they were likely to be shunned rather than applauded, rejected rather than embraced. They faced a man who was a spiritual giant and very much in authority. Sudden exposure, a turn of events to one's disadvantage, and unexpected confrontation: each of these is a situation that tends to produce high anxiety. In their case, it was a triple whammy of anxiety, and the results were profound.

Seek treatment for the root of your anxiety before it deals a deadly blow.

Mark Twain once said, "I have been through some terrible things in my life, some of which actually happened." Many of us spend too much time worrying about the future or worrying about what happened in the past. We then spend much of our lives allowing failures from the past or fears of the future to dominate our thinking.

Philippians 4:6–7 says "Be anxious for nothing, but in everything by prayer and supplication with thanksgiving let your requests be made known unto God; and the peace of God, which surpasses all understanding, will guard your hearts and minds through Christ Jesus."

In Matthew 6, Jesus teaches freedom from anxiety. In verse 25 Jesus says, "Therefore I say to you, do not worry about your life, what you will eat or what you will drink; nor about your body, what you will put on." In verse 34 Jesus said, "Therefore do not worry about tomorrow, for tomorrow will worry about its own things." In other words, live in the present and don't worry about the future or fret about the past. Instead of worrying we should pray and give thanks. An attitude of gratitude and thanksgiving relaxes the body and calms the mind. Follow the advice in 1 Peter 5:7, which says "[cast] all your care upon Him, for He cares for you."

# ┤ 10 ├

# THE WARPING TRAP OF
# RESENTMENT AND BITTERNESS

About eighteen years ago, a petite, middle-aged woman named Lois walked into my office suffering from a mild form of arthritis—specifically, minor joint aches in her fingers. Back then I understood very little about the relationship between nutrition, emotions, lifestyle, and disease. I placed her on a common anti-inflammatory medication and sent her on her way.

Lois's condition improved somewhat for a while, but before long she developed more pain, swelling, and sensations of warmth in her fingers. I ran blood tests and discovered that she had rheumatoid arthritis. I referred her to a rheumatologist.

During Lois's initial physical exam with me, I had asked her about her personal history. She had just been through an ugly, bitter divorce. Her husband of thirty years had left her for another woman who was half her age. The man was quite wealthy, and Lois had gone from living in a mansion and driving a very expensive car to living in a small apartment and driving a secondhand, beat-up automobile. Even so, she was barely able to pay her bills with what she received in the initial maintenance agreement, while the final property settlement was still being negotiated.

Just at the mention of her former husband's name, Lois's soft, sweet countenance and gentle manner changed dramatically. Her face became contorted into a snarl. With deep anger in her low, nearly whispery voice, she told me that she hated her husband and wished him dead. The more she talked, the more her eyes seemed to become smaller and her glare more defiant. She was actually smiling as she told me how much she wanted him to die—and not a peaceful death, either. She wanted him to lose his life painfully and to experience even greater suffering than she had. Rarely had I encountered such deep bitterness and resentment in a patient. Her words chilled the air in the examination room and they troubled me all afternoon.

SHE WAS ACTUALLY SMILING AS SHE TOLD ME HOW MUCH SHE WANTED HIM TO DIE— AND NOT A PEACEFUL DEATH, EITHER.

Certainly, Lois had plenty of reason to be bitter. But reasons do not produce bitterness. Attitudes do. Lois could have made a choice about *how* she would feel about her former husband and her divorce.

The rheumatologist Lois visited placed her on numerous medications for rheumatoid arthritis. She remained under my care as her family physician. Regardless of what the specialist prescribed, Lois's condition only grew worse as the months and years went by.

Within a few years, this once lovely, gentle, gracious woman was bent over, twisted, and contorted. Her face remained frozen in much the same expression I had seen when she first spoke to me so bitterly about her former husband. Her fingers and toes were deformed. Her neck and back were also beginning to twist and flex, leaving her in a most wretched posture.

As we talked in those later years, I realized that her bitterness and resentment had taken over. She lashed out about her husband, even years later, with great vehemence. She perceived that he was the cause of all her pain. She vowed never to forgive him. She told me she still comforted herself at night with images of his suffering in a car wreck in which he was trapped as the vehicle burst into flames. She also said that her only consolation was thinking about how both he and his new wife would burn in hell one day.

When I asked Lois if she thought she would ever be able to forgive her husband, she told me very bluntly, "No. I plan to carry the way I feel to the grave."

Even back then, her ongoing emotional state stunned me, and I had a feeling that the twisted and bitter emotions inside her just might be related to the twisting and contorting of her body. I also knew that I couldn't help her. She rejected my referral to a psychiatrist. She did, indeed, remain extremely bitter until the day she died.

Today, I am firmly convinced that bitterness and unforgiveness may actually have caused Lois's arthritis. Had she made the very difficult choice to forgive her former husband, she may have prevented the devastating pain and suffering that accompanied her physical condition. In the end, her resentment did not hurt her former husband or his new wife nearly as much as they had hurt her . . . literally in both her body and her soul.

Although at present there is no clearly established scientific link between disease and the emotions of resentment, bitterness, and guilt, these emotions nearly always are very closely linked to anger, anxiety, and depression. The latter three are strongly linked to disease. They provoke a strong stress response. I am thoroughly convinced that resentment and bitterness are dimensions of anger: they are the smoldering, lingering ashes of rage and ongoing hostility. I am also thoroughly convinced that much anxiety and depression are rooted in ongoing guilt for which a person has never received genuine forgiveness.

## ANCIENT PEOPLE UNDERSTOOD THIS BETTER!

A glance back in history seems to reveal that the ancients had a much better understanding than we do about the connection between resentment and bitterness and disease. As far back as A.D. 600, Indian medical lore warned healers about attempting to treat those who were filled with toxic emotions. The Ayurvidic Indian text called the *Astangahradaya Sustrasthana* states: "The physician should reject that patient . . . who is busy with other activities . . . who is violent, afflicted with great grief, full of fear."[1]

In other words, the healers believed patients who possessed extremely toxic emotions had a poorer prognosis. They believed these emotions were more powerful than the body's ability to achieve homeostasis, or a healthy balance. They were more potent than any medicines or treatments the Indian healers might prescribe.

Not only do toxic emotions impede the healing process, they compound the effects of sickness by adding new biochemical processes the body must struggle to overcome. This seems especially true when it comes to autoimmune diseases, and rheumatoid arthritis is one of the most painful and progressive forms of an autoimmune disease.

An autoimmune disease begins when the immune system attacks itself. In the military, aggression against one's own forces is called *friendly fire*. The person with an autoimmune disease is a person who is existing in a warlike state of friendly fire.

In an autoimmune disease, the "army" of the body—normally poised to a launch a full-scale attack against invaders such as cancer cells, bacteria, and viruses—loses its ability to discern a true enemy. It begins attacking healthy tissues and organs. Not only that, but it becomes less competent in attacking invaders. An attack against your own body by its own defense system can eventually kill you. The process of death may not happen immediately or even quickly, but over time, the impact can be extremely painful, quite crippling, and ultimately deadly.

- In the case of rheumatoid arthritis, the tissue around the joints (synovium) is attacked and may be eventually destroyed.

- In multiple sclerosis, another autoimmune disease, the myelin sheath, which covers the nerves, is attacked.

- In Hashimoto thyroiditis, the immune system assaults the thyroid gland.

- In psoriasis, the immune system targets the skin.

- In Type 1 diabetes, the islet cells of the pancreas are the goal.

Other autoimmune diseases seem to be more and more prevalent in our society, among them lupus, ulcerative colitis, and Crohn's disease.

With an autoimmune disease, not only does the body see its own tissue as an invader and begin to attack, but a person's general moods and sense of well-being are nearly always affected. That's because the immune system on the attack generates blood proteins called *cytokines,* which are known to induce fatigue and depression.[2]

The brain is able to send both hormonal and nervous signals to suppress the immune system when under stress. When there is a disruption of the regulatory influence of the brain on the immune system, it can lead to increased immune activity and a greater chance of developing inflammatory and autoimmune disease.[3]

Autoimmune disease researchers Sternberg and Gold believe that the brain's ability to regulate itself is also disrupted during an autoimmune attack. This creates even more autoimmune response, which spawns even more inflammation. The downward spiral can be dramatic and frightening.

As we have discussed previously, the brain and the body's immune system communicate in a two-way fashion in an ongoing manner. The brain has the ability to suppress immune function during periods of stress. But when a disruption occurs in the regulatory ability of the brain, the immune activity or immune response can shift into overdrive and remain stuck there. This may very well be the mechanism that leads to autoimmune disease.[4]

And as we have also discussed previously, during periods of stress, glucocorticoids such as cortisol cause a temporary "revving up" of the immune system. The amount of cortisol released over time is a major factor related to immunity. A significant stress event, such as the loss of a loved one, can cause the adrenal glands to secrete a particularly large amount of cortisol. This generally leads to immune suppression, a lowering of immunity in the body.

Ongoing, continuous, more mundane stress, the day-to-day variety, causes the adrenal glands to secrete smaller amounts of cortisol, which actually stimulates the immune system. When this activation of the immune system occurs again and again, an autoimmune disease may result. The body becomes confused—not knowing if it's really necessary to flee or fight, not really sure whom or what to flee from, or whom or what to fight!

God intended that the adrenal glands and the release of cortisol would enable a person to escape traumatic situations and dangerous predators. The body was never supposed to administer cortisol many times throughout the day for minor stresses. The drip, drip, drip effect of smaller doses of cortisol sends the signal "Rev up the immune system! Something *must* be attacking us." When the body cannot find foreign invaders such as viruses and bacteria to attack, the immune system becomes confused and may begin to attack *itself,* causing an autoimmune disease.

Before she died, I truly believe Lois had become entrapped in hate. Her bitterness and resentment had grown to such depths, continually fueled by memories that evoked anger in her, that she not only hated her former husband and his wife, but she hated everything about her life. She hated where and how she lived, how she looked, how she felt physically . . . she hated even herself.

A while before she died, Lois moved away. A relative informed me that she had died in near paralysis—her body had become a prison filled with both physical and emotional pain.

When I received this news from Lois's relative, I couldn't help but feel that Lois's suffering, which had been so severe and so devastating, had been a needless waste. She once had been so attractive and had so much promise, but she allowed her emotions to consume her and rob her of her own potential.

## UNDERSTANDING AND AVOIDING THE HATE TRAP

A strong sense of injustice resulting in bitterness or resentment is frequently mingled with hot anger. The combination is hate, a truly toxic emotion at all times in all persons.

Just as love is the most powerful positive emotion, hatred is the most powerful negative one. Resentment, bitterness, and anger are the dark pathways to this harmful passion.

Many people seem to believe that love and hatred are like the flip sides of a coin that is resident in every person. That simply is not my perception after years of encountering people who were filled with hate. There is very little, if any, love in the person who reflects extreme bitterness, resentment, anger, and hate. Hatred demands more and more emotional space until it crowds out all positive emotions. Raw hate is a fearful and awesome thing to behold in a person. It's as close to evil as I ever hope to get.

> HATRED DEMANDS MORE AND MORE EMOTIONAL
> SPACE UNTIL IT CROWDS OUT ALL
> POSITIVE EMOTIONS.

### Hate Begins with a Grievance

Dr. Fred Luskin is the cofounder and director of the Stanford University Forgiveness Project. In his book, *Forgive for Good,* he documented well the concept of a grievance and its link to hatred and the need to forgive.

A grievance is any circumstance, complaint, or resentment a person thinks is unjust or hurtful. A grievance can be real or imagined. According to Luskin, a grievance occurs when two things coincide:

- Something happens in life that we didn't want to have happen.

- We deal with the problem by thinking about it too much.[5]

When these two things happen simultaneously, we basically rent out too much space in our minds to that particular hurt. Now, if you own an apartment building and you rent out 90 percent of your rooms to gangsters, alcoholics, drug addicts, and robbers, what would happen? In all likelihood, you'd have a host of problems in the building—from damage to the physical facilities to a lessening of the value of the property because of the criminal traffic, not to mention the fact that these undesirable tenants may not be able to pay their rent at the beginning of each month. Destructive tenants not only destroy their own space but all common space. Ultimately, the 10 percent of law-abiding tenants would be responsible for carrying the whole load of financial payment for your building mortgage and repairs.

Sooner or later, you as owner of such a building would either be financially on the rocks or you would be plagued by so many problems that you'd likely abandon the venture.

The same holds true for your emotional well-being, especially when it comes to harboring grievances, grudges, and offenses. When a person rents out too much space to toxic emotions, eventually *all* thoughts are affected, not only those directed toward the offense. A person quickly moves to being cynical, mistrusting, and pessimistic, and in some cases, angry or depressed, at the hurt he has experienced.

People who harbor unforgiveness tend to fume. They exhibit a constant state of irritation, frustration, and hostility. They tend to overreact at the slightest provocation. They spend a dollar's worth of energy on every two-cent problem that comes along. If someone snipes at them at the gas station on the way into work, they can't stop talking about that comment three days later. Negative thoughts churn and churn inside them until negativity consumes them.

Luskin uses the metaphor of a television set, with the person choosing what he will tune in or out. Grudges and offenses are tantamount to horror movies or sex channels. If a person watches too many of those types of programs, the result tends to be inner fear or sexual tension. If a person chooses to watch good programs that portray purity, honesty, justice, strong values, and moral behavior, the person is not only entertained and sometimes educated, but he has a greater sense of overall well-being.

These factors are also present when a person forms a grievance:

- The person takes the grievance too personally.

- The person blames the offender for how he or she feels.

- The person creates a "grievance story" that he or she tells repeatedly.

A grievance story is simply an account of the painful experience from an unhealed past. The story keeps a person stuck in the painful memories. The more he tells or rehearses his story, the more bitterness, resentment, and unforgiveness tend to take root. Each time he shares his account, the feelings of pain, anger, and resentment resurface. The emotional wound never heals because he continually picks at any scab of forgiveness that might form over it.

According to Luskin, the endless loop of grievance stories are actually ineffective attempts to enforce unenforceable rules.

Let me give you an example. One night when I went to a basketball game I parked in a very large parking lot where I was required to pay five dollars to the attendant. Only one attendant was on duty that night, and from across the lot, we could see a stream of cars pouring into the lot from other entrances without paying. The parking attendant had no radio or other means of closing down the entrances so she could stop the freeloaders.

I watched this young woman become increasingly frustrated by this predicament. She kept collecting five dollars from cars, while watching across the lot as others came into the lot without paying. She could not enforce the five-dollar rule and became very agitated.

## WHO MAKES THE RULES

Many times we find ourselves not only the victims of rules we cannot enforce, but we become the creators of such unenforceable rules for others:

- We expect all of our coworkers to talk quietly or not at all . . . at all times.

- We expect our bosses or supervisors to give us credit for everything we do.

- We expect equal rights and equal pay for equal work, the promotions we've earned, and our friends to notice our thoughtful deeds.

- We expect people to meet all their deadlines, to make correct change, our husband or wife to do their share of the housework, and other drivers to mind the traffic signals.

These rules are impossible personally to mandate, and to the extent that we believe the rules *should* be enforceable and kept *all* the time, we will be frustrated and angry.

Sometimes we become extremely frustrated or upset about the rules others seem to set for us. And let's face the fact that we live in a legalistic society. We as a people are rule-oriented. We seem to have rules for everything. I live in a condominium complex that has a neighborhood covenant agreement with more rules than some city charters. I have unknowingly broken some of these rules and been forced to pay fines of hundreds of dollars. Such rules can make a person wonder why he chooses to live in a condominium—ideally, to have less upkeep and yardwork—when the rules seem to be more strenuous than home ownership!

We each run into the rules that others set for us and expect us to obey, even if we aren't aware of those rules. Some people have unspoken rules about what they consider to be polite behavior, how to eat, what is socially acceptable, how their neighbors should keep their lawns, and what is and is not funny.

When others refuse to obey our rules and we have no authority to enforce them, we need to learn how *not* to become frustrated, angry, resentful, or bitter. We need to make a conscious choice that we will *not* sweat the small stuff.

WE NEED TO MAKE A CONSCIOUS CHOICE THAT WE WILL *NOT* SWEAT THE SMALL STUFF.

We also need to make a conscious effort to stop playing traffic cop for the universe. Not everybody's rules or standards will ever be the same as yours. The best you can do is to live up to your own standards and let others live up to theirs.

## GETTING TO THE CORE OF INJUSTICE

Anger related to unenforceable rules easily spills over into bitterness, hostility, and ongoing resentment. It transforms from a *hot* anger related to the situation of the moment into a *seething* anger that becomes an ongoing offense. Each time we recall the insult, we add another layer of anger to the accumulated mound of offense. Over time, resentment and bitterness grow stronger and stronger. These are not emotions that diminish over time.

### The Blame Game

The blame game is certainly a part of ongoing bitterness and resentment. The person who is feeling bitter nearly always believes that someone else is at fault. It may be the spouse who committed adultery, the mother-in-law who pushed for the divorce, the father who was abusive, or the boss who was unreasonable. At times people blame God. The bitter person truly believes God should have stopped the husband from leaving, the father from abusing, or the fire from destroying the house.

A continual ruminating about past injustices causes the feelings of injustice to remain. And since additional negative circumstances may arise in the wake of that divorce, abuse, fire, and so forth, the sense of injustice only deepens.

Perhaps the most common statements of a bitter person are:

- "I didn't deserve this."

- "This shouldn't have happened to me."

- "This wasn't fair."

The common statements a resentful person makes are:

- "I *did* deserve the good thing, but somebody else got what I deserved." The "good thing" may be a reward, a promotion, a raise, or some other visible awarding of recognition and value.

- "Nobody appreciates who I am or what I have done."

- "I'm overworked and underpaid."

I have had countless patients come to me with their depression or other emotional and physical ailments, saying,

- "If only my coworker hadn't told on me for being late, my boss wouldn't have fired me." Never mind that the person was late ninety days out of the last one hundred.

- "If only my professor had liked me, I wouldn't have failed the course and had to delay graduating, which meant I was subject to the military draft, and therefore I suffered through the war, never finished college, and my life was ruined." Never mind that this former student hadn't studied, attended lectures, or turned in the required assignments.

- "If only my spouse hadn't divorced me, I would have had a wonderful life." Never mind that life with that spouse was far from wonderful.

People who play the blame game don't just blame another person for a past failure or event, but they continue to blame the person for current failures and negative experiences. Long after the perpetrator has had any direct role in the person's life, the blamer continues to point his finger at the person and say, "Anything that goes wrong in my life is your fault." I once heard a media interview with a man who had beaten his wife to death. He took no responsibility for his own actions, saying, "She just pushed me too far that time."

Those who become expert at the blame game become psychologically dependent upon the person they are blaming. They perceive themselves as powerless to fix or change any painful situation they encounter. That lack of power opens up a person to depression.

*Blaming God*

As I mentioned, some people do not blame others or themselves as much as they blame God for what has happened to them.

Through the years I have met a number of people who admit to me, somewhat reluctantly and usually after a lengthy conversation, that they are mad at God. They blame God for the death of the spouse from cancer, the good job they lost, or the unfortunate accident that left them disfigured, crippled, or scarred. Some people blame God for *all* the bad they have suffered in life.

The Bible teaches that good and bad happen to human beings. Life is not always fair. Sometimes good people experience pain and suffering. Sometimes bad people experience great material wealth or enjoy positions of power and prestige. God's promise is never that those who serve Him will avoid all pain or hard times, but rather that His presence will be with those who obey Him, *at all times.* He promises to help us in our times of need. He promises to bring us through the "valley of the shadow" and to prepare for us the future He desires for us (see Ps. 23; John 14:1–4).

What should you do if you feel anger or resentment toward God? Tell Him what you feel! The Bible has no examples of God condemning people who expressed anger toward Him. As one woman said, "God has shoulders big enough to take any expression of anger or resentment we give to Him."

---

WHAT SHOULD YOU DO IF YOU FEEL ANGER OR RESENTMENT TOWARD GOD? TELL HIM WHAT YOU FEEL!

---

Job is a person in the Bible who expressed his deepest feelings to God, including confusion, pain, and anger. The psalmist David wrote repeatedly of the ways in which he felt God had afflicted his soul.

Once you have thoroughly vented your feelings to God, ask God to help you trust Him "even in this." The Bible tells us that "all things work together for good to those who love God, to those who are the called according to His purpose" (Rom. 8:28). We may not be able to see any good purpose in what we have experienced, but we must recognize that we see with finite eyes that are limited to the here and now. God sees with infinite eyes throughout the span of eternity.

## A RELATIONSHIP BETWEEN ENVY
## AND RESENTMENT

There's a close link between being envious of a person and resenting that person. We generally call envy by another name: *jealousy.*

Have you ever felt jealous? It is a terrible feeling that can totally rob you of joy. Jealousy is a painful or resentful awareness of the advantage that another person is enjoying. It is coupled with an intense desire to possess that same advantage. Jealousy readily leads to feelings of rivalry or vengeance, which in turn can lead to anger and hostility.

Jealousy tends to be an all-consuming emotion, not unlike depression or hostility. Jealousy eats at a person and taints all he does and sees.

Many people believe they are jealous because they love a person and don't want anybody else to have even an acquaintanceship or friendship with him or her. The Bible, however, says this: "Love does not envy" (1 Cor. 13:4).

The Bible also says:

- A sound heart is life to the body,
  But envy is rottenness to the bones. (Prov. 14:30)

- For wrath kills a foolish man,
  And envy slays a simple one. (Job 5:2)

- Now the works of the flesh are evident, which
  [include] . . . envy. (Gal. 5:19, 21)

- Do not let your heart envy sinners. (Prov. 23:17)

- Do not be envious of evil men,
  Nor desire to be with them. (Prov. 24:1)

Repeatedly the writers of the New Testament warned against envy. They noted that it led to "confusion and every evil thing" (see James 3:13–16; Gal. 5:26; Rom. 13:13 as examples). They saw envy in contrast to wisdom and associated it with bitterness.

Jealousy easily leads to anger, hostility, bitterness, depression, and other toxic emotions.

## THE CRYING NEED FOR FORGIVENESS

A person finds a cure for both envy and the blame game associated with resentment only when he is willing to forgive the one who has offended him.

Recently a man and his wife came into my office. Rodney was experiencing heart palpitations and severe eczema that was covering his face, hands, back, and legs. He was very uncomfortable. Edna, his tall, blonde wife, was experiencing chronic fatigue and fibromyalgia.

We began to talk about the totality of their lives, and it didn't take long before I could begin to put the pieces of their emotional picture into place. Rodney was an executive for a major computer company. He traveled a great deal. Edna stayed at home to care for their two young children. While Rodney was gone, Edna, a Christian woman and leader in her church, began having an affair with a young Cuban gardener.

Rodney, who was extremely fair, with alabaster skin and bright-red hair, became suspicious when their young son was born with dark brown skin and jet-black hair. Weeping uncontrollably one evening, Edna confessed to her affair and resulting pregnancy. Rodney was devastated.

Rodney had blamed Edna for everything that went wrong in their lives prior to the affair and after it, and for the pain they were in. He had accepted the child as his own but barely spoke to his wife after her confession. For the most part, he had buried his jealousy, anger, and grief deep within his heart, where it remained locked and festering for two years. Edna, on the other hand, had buried herself in deep humiliation and shame.

Before I prescribed something to each of them for their physical symptoms, I had the opportunity to lead them in a prayer of release. I encouraged them, with God's help, to let go of their pent-up toxic emotions, to release the past hurt, and to seek to forgive each other and themselves.

What happened in the next few minutes was astonishing.

Both of them began to weep, then sob. In moments they were both shaking and nearly wailing as a flood of emotions poured out of their hearts. Afterward, they spent some time forgiving themselves and each other for the hurt they had caused.

By the time this couple left my office, they looked like new people. Their eyes were brighter; the gray color of their complexions had changed. There was a sense of calm in their expressions and demeanor. Both of them made a commitment to roll up their sleeves, figuratively speaking, and work on a change in their distorted thought patterns. They made a mutual decision to seek healing and freedom from their pain—physically, emotionally, and spiritually.

As their physician, I was thrilled. I had a strong feeling that their physical healing would be close at hand . . . and it was. After they first addressed and released the toxic emotions that had been brewing inside them, they were both completely free of all the symptoms that had brought them to my office.

## STOPPING A GRIEVANCE FROM DEVELOPING

I often say to people, "Hate is a preventable disease." You can keep a grievance from taking root in your emotional soul.

If you find yourself fuming about a particular situation, ask yourself:

- "Why does this upset me so much?" Was there an unenforceable rule involved in this situation? Question whether your assumptions about the behavior of others is at the root of your response.

- "What choice do I have if another person chooses to disobey this unenforceable rule?" This is not a question that should lead you to feel that you have no power to influence others, but rather, it is a question designed to trigger thoughts of alternatives to getting angry or feeling frustrated.

Quickly move toward releasing your frustration. Refuse to dwell on the other person's behavior.

You may not be able to change a situation or another person's behavior, but you can choose to *respond* to that behavior in a way that promotes your own emotional well-being and physical health.

*Let It Fly on By*
A woman once shared this story with me: Her grandmother had begun to suffer dementia, and her family placed her in a nursing

home. In younger years, the grandmother had never spoken abusively or critically to her daughter, much less uttered obscenities or foul language. Suddenly these behaviors were occurring and when confronted about them, the grandmother had absolutely no memory that she had said such things. She seemed shocked that others would use "such language" in her presence.

The daughter of this woman with dementia was very upset at the change in her mother. The granddaughter—the woman sharing the story with me—was a little more objective. She said to her mother one day, "Mom, you've just got to let some things fly right on by"—and she made a little flying gesture with her hands. The mother laughed and agreed that was the right response.

Over the course of the next two years until the grandmother died, daughter and granddaughter shared a number of occasions in which they simply looked at each other and made that little flying gesture. The granddaughter said to me, "It was our shorthand for saying, 'This isn't worth remembering. This isn't who Grandma really is. We can't hold on to this or let it hurt us. We just have to let it fly on by.'"

Then the granddaughter said, "Long after Grandma died, Mom and I still used that little shorthand to remind each other that insults, critical comments, and angry words just aren't worth holding on to. Even when someone cut us off in traffic or gave us an obscene gesture, well, we'd just give each other the fly-on-by sign. One day I asked Mom what she thought of a particular sermon she had just heard on television and she gave me the fly-on-by sign. The sign also worked for bad theology that shouldn't be internalized!"

### Take a Positive Step

Not only should you choose to let some things fly on by, or choose to ignore the offending behavior, but you need to take a *positive* step to keep the grievance from taking root.

Whistle or hum a tune. Play a CD or tape, or tune in your favorite oldies radio station and sing along!

Turn your mind to something positive that requires some concentration. Experts on aging are telling us that one of the best ways to keep the mind alive into older years is to continue to learn and memorize positive quotes, poems, Bible verses, and songs. Pull out something that you are currently learning and memorizing and practice reciting the passage.

You might also set your mind to the planning of a particular task—something totally unrelated to the person or offense you have just experienced. For example, if you are redecorating your daughter's bedroom, planning a party, or designing a new patio deck, begin to think about it and then list, sketch, or make notes about that project.

Respond immediately to help someone in need. Turn an act of offense or a grievance against you into an act of loving generosity.

*Les Misérables* is a book, movie, and stage musical that has impacted literally millions of people since it was first published. The main character, Jean Valjean, is condemned unjustly for stealing a loaf of bread to feed his starving family. Upon his release from prison, hardened by the injustice and years of hard labor, he steals silver from a priest who gives him a meal and shelter. When Jean is caught with the items, the priest refuses to accuse him of stealing and loads his knapsack with even more silver.

This one act of mercy changes Valjean's life forever. He becomes a man of mercy and benevolence.

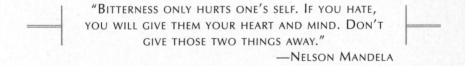

"BITTERNESS ONLY HURTS ONE'S SELF. IF YOU HATE, YOU WILL GIVE THEM YOUR HEART AND MIND. DON'T GIVE THOSE TWO THINGS AWAY."
—NELSON MANDELA

The best antidote for an offense against us is to respond by committing an act of benevolence or generosity toward someone else. In doing so, you are choosing to rent out more space in your heart to love than to unforgiveness, hate, anger, bitterness, or any other toxic emotion.

Refuse to give away your health—emotional and physical. Former South African President Nelson Mandela, when asked how he survived years of imprisonment without growing bitter, replied, "Bitterness only hurts one's self. If you hate, you will give them your heart and mind. Don't give those two things away."[6] I couldn't agree more.

# Part II

# THE PRESCRIPTION

## CLAIMING
## HEALTHY EMOTIONS

# ─┤ 11 ├─

# MAKING THE CHOICE FOR HEALTH

Victor Frankl was a psychiatrist and a Jew. Nazis imprisoned him in the death camps of World War II Germany, where he experienced things so repugnant to a normal person's sense of decency that he could scarcely reduce them to words.

Frankl's parents, brother, and wife died in the camps or were murdered in the gas ovens. Of his immediate family, only his sister survived the camps. Frankl himself suffered torture and innumerable indignities, never knowing from one moment to the next if his captors would send him to the ovens or leave him among those who were "saved" and left with the task of removing the bodies or shoveling out the ashes of those who had been cremated while they were still alive.

One day, naked and alone in a small room, Frankl began to become aware of what he later called "the last of the human freedoms"—the one freedom his Nazi captors could not take away. Frankl openly acknowledged that the Nazis could control his entire environment and do what they wanted with his body. They could not, however, destroy his inner identity. He saw himself as a self-aware human being who had an ability to be a somewhat objective observer of his situation. He still had the power within himself to determine how his outer circumstances and the Nazis' treatment of him were going to affect his inner self. He saw that there was a gap between what happened to him (the stimulus) and his reaction to the stimulus (response), and that in that gap lay the freedom or power to *choose* a response.[1]

Frankl came face-to-face with the reality that his own *choices,* not his circumstances, defined his identity. No matter how horrifying the environment in which he lived, and no matter how much humiliation and degradation others heaped upon him, he was still in control of how he chose to respond.

The same is true for each one of us.

No matter what you may have been through, even unspeakable pain, you are still in control of your identity. No event can change you on the inside unless you allow it to do so. No person can cause you to respond in a particular way on the inside unless you choose to react that way. The freedom to forge your own opinions, ideas, attitudes, and choices rests solely and uniquely with *you.*

## THE POWER OF YOUR ATTITUDE

I recently read a short essay on attitude by Charles Swindoll. He wrote:

> Words can never adequately convey the incredible impact of our attitude toward life. The longer I live the more convinced I become that life is 10 percent what happens to us and 90 percent how we respond to it.
>
> I believe the single most significant decision I can make on a day-to-day basis is my choice of attitude. It is more important than my past, my education, my bankroll, my successes or failures, fame or pain, what other people think of me or say about me, my circumstances, or my position. Attitude keeps me going or cripples my progress. It alone fuels my fire or assaults my hope. When my attitudes are right, there's no barrier too high, no valley too deep, no dream too extreme, no challenge too great for me.
>
> *Stengthening Your Grip*
> by CHARLES R. SWINDOLL
> Insight for Living, www.insight.org
> (Nashville, Tenn.: W Publishing Group, 1982), pp. 206–7
> Used by permission of Insight for Living, Plano, TX 75026

All deadly emotions, to some extent, derive from our attitudes. And attitudes are something we can control. You can choose how you will think and feel about any circumstance, event, or relationship in your life. You can choose to a very great extent how you deal with grief, resentment, bitterness, shame, jealousy, guilt, fear, worry, depression, anger, hostility, and all other emotional situations that readily trigger physical responses.

The first step you need to take toward health is to reflect upon your own attitudes. Own up to the attitudes you have. Ask yourself, "Is this the way I *want* to think and believe?"

## CHECK IN WITH YOUR REAL SELF

As we discussed in an earlier chapter, your "heart" is the real you.

Even before the brain of a fetus forms, a tiny heart begins to beat. Scientists don't know what makes it begin its long journey of beating for seventy, eighty, or more years. Medical practitioners use the word *autorhythmic* to describe how a heart begins beating all by itself.

While the source of the heart's beating is found within the heart itself, researchers believe the brain controls the timing of each beat. Even so, a heart does not need to be "hardwired" to the brain to continue a steady, rhythmical beating. When a surgeon is harvesting a heart for transplantation, he severs the nerves running to the deceased person's brain. He then places the heart into another person's chest and restores the beat. Surgeons do not know how to reconnect the nerves of the newly installed heart to the brain, so a connection between the two organs is lost, at least temporarily. Nevertheless, the new heart that is jump-started continues to beat, beat, beat.

How can this be? In recent years neuroscientists have discovered that the heart has its own independent nervous system. At least forty thousand nerve cells (neurons) exist in a human heart. That's the same amount found in various subcortical (beneath the cerebral cortex) centers of the brain.[2] In other words, the heart is more than a mere biological pump. These abundant nerve cells give it a thinking, feeling capability.

The heart's "brain" and the nervous system relay messages back and forth to the brain in the skull, creating a two-way communication between these two organs. In the 1970s physiologists John and Beatrice Lacey of the Fels Research Institute found a flaw in current popular thinking about the brain. The popular approach was to assume that the brain made all of the body's decisions. The Laceys' research indicated otherwise.

Specifically, these researchers found that while the brain may send instructions to the heart through the nervous system, the heart doesn't automatically obey. Instead, the heart seems to respond at times as if it is "considering" the information that it has received. Sometimes when the brain sends an arousal signal to the body in response to external stimuli, the heart speeds up, as might be expected. On other occasions, however, the heart slows down while all other organs are aroused as expected.

The selectivity of the heart's response suggested to the Laceys that the heart does not mechanically respond to the brain's signals. Rather, the heart seems to have an opinion of its own, which it communicates back to the brain.

What was even more interesting in the Laceys' research was the fact that the messages that the heart sent to the brain seemed to be ones that the brain not only understood but obeyed. In effect, heart and brain hold an intelligent dialogue. At times the heart submits to the brain, and on other occasions the brain seems to submit to the heart. The messages from the heart appear to be capable of affecting an individual's behavior.[3]

The ultimate "real you" is a composite of what your heart tells your brain, your brain tells your heart, and your will decides to believe, say, and do.

## COMMUNICATING WITH YOUR OWN HEART

Two of the most powerful antidotes I know for toxic emotions are these:

- Communicating with your own heart
- Learning to live in the love that flows from the heart

King David talked to his own heart. He asked of himself, "Why are you cast down, O my soul? And why are you disquieted within me? Hope in God, for I shall yet praise Him for the help of His countenance" (Ps. 42:5).

You may feel silly "talking to your heart," but do it anyway! Voice to yourself what it is that you are feeling most deeply. Just venting the words will do two things: it will clarify to you what you truly are feeling, and you will give release to some of your pent-up emotions.

Notice that David did not only admit to himself that he was downcast in his soul. He went on to tell himself, "Hope in God!" He went on to say of his chosen course of action, "I shall yet praise Him." Furthermore, David said he would praise God for the "help of His countenance." He praised God not for a specific act that God had taken or would take, but for the sheer help of knowing that God was present with him.

These three steps David took in his "soul conversation" are very important. You can follow his lead:

1. Admit to yourself—speaking aloud—what it is that you are feeling.

2. Voice aloud your decision to hope in God.

3. Voice aloud your decision to praise God for who He is in your life. Acknowledge His near presence and His continual availability to you.

David went on to voice these same concepts to God in prayer: "O my God, my soul is cast down within me; therefore I will remember You" (Ps. 42:6).

Turn from speaking to yourself to speaking to God. Admit to God your feelings. Cast your concerns on Him and voice your decision to trust Him—to remember that He is with you and will always be faithful to you.

What is required for effective communication with your heart? You must become quiet and do your best to turn off the constant mental tapes that are playing in your head, to turn away from the remembrance of painful hurts and frustrations. The heart speaks in a quiet whisper. Many people find it helpful to focus on events or people in their lives that have brought joy, love, happiness, and peace. Also develop an attitude of gratitude and appreciation by focusing on all the good things in your life rather than the traumas or negative things that have happened.

THE HEART SPEAKS IN A QUIET WHISPER.

Ask your heart:

- "What is it that you are *really* feeling?"

- "*Why* are you *really* feeling this way?"

- "What good thing are you *really* hoping for?"

- "What good thing do you want to see done?"

The heart speaks in the quietest of voices. You may feel a little internal "nudge" or a sense of warning. Give your heart the benefit of communicating its wisdom to your brain.

I cannot tell you how many of my cancer patients tell me they "just knew" they had cancer even before they were diagnosed. In contrast, I've had patients tell me they were so afraid they had cancer, even though deep down inside they didn't believe it was really so, that they seemed surprised when a physician told them they were healthy. These people had allowed fear to cloud the messages from their own hearts. I encourage you to spend a few minutes every day listening to your heart. And then:

- Speak words of encouragement to your heart.

- Voice words of appreciation for life's blessings—words of thanks and praise to God.

- Recall events in your life when you experienced tremendous joy, peace, or love.

- Speak words of acknowledgment about personal accomplishments, reflections of noble character, or acts of kindness or ministry to others. If nobody else openly acknowledges the goodness of the Lord manifested in and through your life, acknowledge this to yourself.

- Read aloud the Word of God to your heart. I recommend that you place an emphasis on the words of Jesus in the New Testament, the book of Proverbs, and the books of 1, 2, and 3 John.

- Voice your heartfelt prayers and concerns to God, beginning with a time of giving God thanks for all He has done, is doing, and has promised to do. Speak your praise to God for who He is.

- Give God your frustrations, fears, and anger. Turn over your anxious thoughts to Him. The Bible tells us, "Let [God] have all your worries and cares, for he is always thinking about you and watching everything that concerns you" (1 Peter 5:7 TLB).

- Ask God to fill your heart with His love and presence. Openly invite the Holy Spirit to impart to you the fruit of His presence in you, which includes "love, joy, peace, longsuffering, kindness, goodness, faithfulness, gentleness, self-control" (Gal. 5:22–23).

When you experience God in your heart, you will also experience His love. The Bible says the two are inseparable: "He who does not love does not know God, for God is love" (1 John 4:8).

## IS YOUR RELATIONSHIP WITH GOD
## IN YOUR HEAD OR HEART?

Pastor Jack Frost has spoken eloquently about having a heart relationship with God. He contrasts this with having a "mind experience with doctrine," which leads a person to become judgmental and legalistic. Legalism is cold and harsh compared to the warmth and wonder of divine love.

Frost's father was a stern, rejecting man who was impossible to please. Frost perceived that God operated in the same way. He continually sought to win God's approval and love in the ways he had sought his father's. Instead, he found what he calls "cold abandonment."

Eventually Frost's own family fell into a serious crisis time. His wife became deeply depressed. His children exhibited numerous behavioral problems. His own heart was warped by cold judgmentalism and legalism.

Then one day as Frost was crying out to God, the Spirit of God ministered to him in an amazing way. Frost lay on the floor as wave after wave of God's love swept over him. He wept uncontrollably for quite a time as God's love pushed the hidden core of pain to the surface of his heart and then washed it away.

When Frost finally stood up, he was a new man. He said, "I had a radical encounter with Jesus that changed the moral issues of my life." He felt in touch with his own heart for the first time in many years. He saw his heavenly Father as loving and in turn, he felt love instead of fear, rejection, judgment, bitterness, or pain. In those moments of supernatural "heart-soaking," the pendulum of his heart and God's own beating heart fell into a synchronized rhythm.[4]

I have had a number of patients who grew up with a father similar to Jack Frost's. They have rehearsed tales of criticism, judgment, and hate that at times have made me feel great disgust and sadness on their behalf. Some of these fathers have told their children, verbally or nonverbally, that they were and are stupid, worthless, and incapable of any form of genuine achievement.

Every child has the basic need to be loved without condition—to be loved simply because he *is,* solely because he is a creation God entrusted to this earth. Infants who are held, kissed, and hugged on a regular basis are usually much healthier emotionally than those who are held infrequently. Touching is a vital component of thriving for an infant and young child.

## THE PHYSIOLOGICAL COMMUNICATION OF THE HEART TO THE BODY

As you learn to communicate with your own heart and release positive feelings of love to your own soul, your heart in turn communicates this message of well-being to your body through the release of helpful hormones and neurotransmitters. The most powerful channel of heart communication to the body, however, is through the heart's electromagnetic field, which is about five thousand times greater in strength than the electromagnetic field the brain produces.[5]

Scientists are able to detect electronic information the heart sends through a brain-wave test called an electroencephalogram (EEG). Gary Schwartz and his colleagues at the University of Arizona found in their experiments that neurological or other established communication pathways could explain the complex patterns of cardiac activity in our brain waves. In other words, acting somewhat like military code breakers in World War II, these researchers had to learn "the language of the heart." Their data showed the existence of direct energetic interaction between the electromagnetic field of the heart and that produced by the brain.

In addition, heart rates tended to send varying messages to the brain and body.[6] When a person is fearful, for example, the heart speeds up, sending a signal to the entire body. When a person is content and happy, heart rate slows, telling the entire nervous system that the person is feeling good.

A seventeenth-century clock maker discovered a fascinating principle that we can apply to this matter of the heart's beating. Christiaan Huygens invented the pendulum clock, and with great pride he manufactured a collection of his clocks to sell. One day as he lay in bed, staring at his clock collection on the other side of the room, he noticed that all of the pendulums were swinging in unison, even though he knew with certainty they hadn't started out that way.

Huygens got out of bed and restarted the pendulums, purposefully setting them at different times to break the synchronized rhythm. To his amazement, in fairly short order, the pendulums began swinging together again.

Later, scientists discovered that it was the largest clock with the strongest rhythm that was pulling the other pendulums into sync with itself. They gave this phenomenon the name "entrainment,"[7] which is apparent throughout nature.

The fact is, the strongest biological oscillator in the body is the heart. It acts in a way similar to Huygens's clocks. The heart has the ability to pull every other bodily system into its own rhythm, whatever that may be. When the heart is at peace or filled with love, it communicates harmony to the entire body. And conversely, when toxic emotions have triggered the heart to beat in an irregular way, to beat harder, or to beat faster, the heart communicates the very opposite of peace to the other organs of the body.

WHEN THE HEART IS AT PEACE OR FILLED WITH LOVE, IT COMMUNICATES HARMONY TO THE ENTIRE BODY.

Spiritually speaking, when you experience God's peace, the heart communicates peace to every fiber of your being. Each and every organ experiences that rest. When a person experiences God's love and the love of other people, the heart in similar fashion communicates that love to his mind and to his entire body. When love fills your heart, your entire body takes something of an emotional plunge into healing.

The greatest Physician and Healer who ever lived, Jesus Christ, explained this phenomenon in His own terms: "It is not what goes into a man that defiles a man, but what comes out of his heart" (Matt. 15:16–18, author's paraphrase).

A patient named Hal came to me because he was experiencing palpitations in his heart. I told him that each time he had one of these episodes, he needed to stop and listen to his heart instead of his head, which was telling him he was having a heart attack and he needed to get to the hospital as soon as possible. I said to Hal, "Take a daily 'heart-soak.'" By that I meant that Hal needed to get into a quiet place of prayer each day and allow his heart to experience the things that it desired: gentle moments, quiet gratitude, small pleasures. I instructed Hal to spend at least ten minutes a day "soaking" his heart in the things he loved.

One thing Hal loved greatly was his youngest grandson, Josh. Josh adored Hal and mimicked everything he did. In his time of "heart-soaking," Hal began pulling thoughts and feelings from deep inside his heart that were identical to the thoughts and feelings he had when Josh visited him. I encouraged him to savor the pleasure of those experiences and to begin thanking God one by one for each and every precious encounter he had enjoyed with his grandson.

Soon, every time Hal's stress began to trigger palpitations, he was able to pull Josh's photo out of his wallet, get in touch with his heart, and quietly thank God for this precious child. He and his wife, Frances, started taking walks together in the woods, something they had done when they were dating. Hal loved the smell of moist earth in the woods and the grand elegance of the chestnut trees growing on his property. In fact, he had initially purchased the property for its trees, but somehow through the years he had forgotten to appreciate their beauty and grandeur.

It wasn't long before Hal's heart palpitations stopped. More important to Hal, however, was the fact that he had learned to enjoy his life again. He had learned to listen to his own heart.

Begin to practice an attitude of gratitude and appreciation. In Philippians 4:4, Paul says, "Rejoice in the Lord always. Again I will say rejoice." Paul was writing to the church in Philippi, which was a Roman colony. Paul, however, wrote this letter from prison. Judgment for Paul was imminent, and conditions were harsh for him, and yet Paul also wrote from prison in Ephesians 5:20, "giving thanks always for all things to God the Father in the name of our Lord Jesus Christ." Where the mind goes, the health of your body will follow. If your mind is full of anxiety, fear, anger, depression, and guilt it chronically stimulates the stress response which opens the door for disease to enter the body. I believe that many diseases, such as autoimmune disease and cancer, are directly related to deadly emotions. It's like deadly emotions are flipping a self-destruct switch in your body.

Start practicing appreciation and thanksgiving on a daily basis. Compliment your wife, children, coworkers, and friends regularly. Begin to compliment or give words of appreciation to strangers such as waiters, store clerks, toll-booth operators, and people that you come in contact with daily. Instead of pointing out their faults, begin to see their strengths. I remember complimenting a toll-booth operator for the great job he was doing and how his line moved faster than all the others. His face beamed with pride. Most people yearn for others to acknowledge and recognize the good job that they are doing. It is true that people will work harder for recognition than for money.

---┤ 12 ├---

# REPLACING DISTORTIONAL
# THINKING WITH TRUTH

People avoided Milt, and it was no wonder. In a crowded, busy restaurant Milt was known to pull his shirt out of his slacks, unzip his trousers, and show off his abdominal scars from various surgical procedures. No matter how a conversation with him started, he eventually ended it with one or more of his many tales of "rare and unusual diseases" he had experienced.

After nearly two decades of diligent effort to convince the bureaucrats associated with disabilities that he really was "dying" of emphysema, Milt finally won his case. He was absolutely delighted over the fact that the government had affirmed his state of chronic sickness, and he rarely stopped talking about it.

Agnes was similar in some respects, although her chronic diseases were different. She was a very short, extremely obese woman who scheduled her week around visits to chiropractors, doctors, massage therapists, various medical specialists, and other people she hoped would help her feel better. Only in her early thirties, she looked and acted much older. People often mistook her for a retired person. After years of visits to a long list of medical-care providers, she had finally received a diagnosis of chronic fatigue, arthritis, and fibromyalgia. She wore that diagnosis like a badge of honor. She spoke of little else.

I encountered Milt and Agnes shortly after I began my medical practice, and frankly, they puzzled me. I had never before encountered people who didn't seem to want to get well. I did not know the phrase *distortional thinking* at that time, but in retrospect, they were definitely suffering from that condition. Through the years, I've discovered that between a third and a half of all my patients with chronic diseases who don't seem to *want* to get well, have distorted thinking about their ailments. Their identities seem clouded by toxic emotions that arise from a warped and broken belief system.

Some people seem to develop distortional thinking at an early age. One patient of mine was only twenty-five years old when she became chronically ill. Her illness began shortly after her husband announced his homosexual desires and told her he wanted to leave her to pursue male companionship. Her subsequent chronic illness had kept her guilty mate close at hand to care for her during her bad days. With chronic migraines, chronic back pain, chronic TMJ pain, and an ever-growing list of complaints, she confessed to me that her bad days were now every day.

## WHAT IS DISTORTIONAL THINKING?

Years ago a *Pogo* comic strip became popular because it so accurately and succinctly described the human condition. Pogo declared, "We have met the enemy and they are us!"

Sadly, we are often our own worst enemies when we take into our beings the very ideas and beliefs that hurt us far more than help us.

Psychological and psychiatric literature sometimes calls distortional thinking *psychological reversal*. It is a condition in which the patient says he wants to get well, but subconsciously he does not. Psychologists and psychiatrists have long known that some patients have self-defeating natures. They resist treatment in a variety of ways. They forget to take their prescribed medications or refuse to take them because they "don't like the aftertaste." They insist they are not responding to treatment even when their symptoms improve. They may stop a particular program of treatment just when it seems to be working for them.

The reasons for self-sabotage are many and varied. One of the more obvious is the following:

## "I Am My Disease"

Some individuals grow up with a disease or they have experienced the illness for such a long period of time that they form their personal identity around it. Their point of uniqueness is the disease or ailment they have. This was likely the case with Milt and Agnes.

In individuals such as these, illness becomes their way of life. Milt did not see himself as Milt. He saw himself as Emphysema Milt. Such individuals do not perceive that they are people with normal lives who happen to get ill, but as ill people who do normal things that are all focused on a remote possibility they might become well.

> MILT DID NOT SEE HIMSELF AS MILT. HE SAW HIMSELF AS EMPHYSEMA MILT.

In some ways, their illnesses become an exchange for jobs they hate, the drudgery of housework and other chores, and boring, loveless relationships. When you ask a person who has this form of distortional thinking, "What do you do for fun?" he often responds with a blank stare. The fact is, they don't have hobbies or careers. They don't have any pastimes other than talking about their ailment.

Any time you hear a person use such phrases as "my arthritis," "my chronic pain," or "my multiple sclerosis," you have a clue that the person has so adopted this ailment or disease that he is starting to identify himself inseparably with it.

The vast majority of these people who see themselves as infirmities also have infirm careers. In other words, they don't work. As contrasted with people who genuinely are disabled in some way or who are physically unable to work for a legitimate reason, they believe, either consciously or subconsciously, that their diseases entitle them to all forms of charitable and government assistance. They see entitlement payments as a reward for having the illness.

They delight in perks they don't necessarily need or deserve, from the handicapped parking sticker to recognition as being part of a class-action lawsuit. Those who receive extra love, money, excitement, or esteem from their illness rarely have a strong desire or commitment to getting well.

Not long ago a woman came from Mexico to my office. She was loaded with toxic emotions. She came in carrying a suitcase filled with the vitamins and other supplements she was taking. She was livid at the cabdriver who had brought her from the airport to my office. When she began unloading on him the reason for her visit to the United States, he had replied, "Your problem is that you don't really want to get well." In my opinion, he had hit the nail on the head.

I spent a week helping this woman identify and change her distortional belief systems. By the time she left she reported feeling better. I hope those feelings lasted. She had been a bundle of negative life beliefs.

## NEGATIVE LIFE BELIEFS

Dr. James Durlacher has written:

> Negative life beliefs generally come from some real or imagined remark, pronouncement or anything else said to, or overheard by, the person—usually coming from someone in authority. This authority is usually a parent but can be a relative, teacher, clergyman/woman, police officer, employer, employee, or anyone else whom the person regards as authoritative or knowledgeable.[1]

When we are stressed, depressed, angry, anxious, or feeling guilty, we become more prone to misinterpreting events and to thinking in a distorted way. One distorted thought tends to lead to another and, before long, we are trapped in a downward spiral. We begin voicing negative statements such as:

- "Nothing ever goes right for me."

- "I just can't do anything right."

- "Everything I touch fails."

Two of the leading pioneers in this area are Dr. Albert Ellis and Dr. Aaron Beck.

Dr. Ellis, a renowned psychologist in the 1950s, developed a form of psychotherapy called *rational emotive therapy*. Dr. Ellis believed that toxic emotions arise from three negative and incorrect beliefs:

Wrong Belief #1: I must do well.

Wrong Belief #2: You must treat me well.

Wrong Belief #3: The world must be easy.[2]

A sane, rational, and potentially positive person is someone who recognizes that nobody does well *all* the time. Everybody has faults, foibles, and flaws. The healthy perception is that people at times are *not* going to treat us well, and the world at times is *not* going to be easy.

In the 1960s Dr. Beck developed cognitive therapy, in which the patient learns to change his way of thinking and the way he interprets events. A significant part of the therapy involves changing the way a person *talks*.

In response to a negatively perceived situation, a person in cognitive therapy might be taught to say:

- "This didn't go well, but most of the time things do go well."

- "I may have made a mistake this time, but I can do lots of things well."

- "I may have failed in this, but overall I've enjoyed successes in my life."[3]

One of the experts in cognitive therapy is Dr. David Burns, a renowned psychiatrist and author of the best-selling book *Feeling Good*. Dr. Burns has conducted more than thirty thousand cognitive therapy sessions in his career and he sees these principles as vital for a person to gain control over his own toxic beliefs and negative thinking patterns:

- Your thoughts create your moods. *Cognition* actually refers to beliefs, perceptions, and mental attitudes, and how you interpret events. These thoughts can create the emotions of anger, hostility, depression, sadness, anxiety, fear, shame, or guilt.

- When a person feels depressed, his thoughts are dominated by negativity.

- The negative thoughts linked to emotional turmoil nearly always contain major distortions. These distortions might also be called *irrational, twisted,* or *unrealistic* thought patterns.[4]

Dr. Burns has identified ten types of negative beliefs:

### 1. All-or-Nothing Thinking

The person who thinks this way sees everything in black-or-white terms. No shades of gray are possible. Perfectionists see their work as either perfect or worthless. The healthy person sees spectrums and variations and exceptions in nearly every area of life.

### 2. Overgeneralizations

This is the tendency to draw sweeping conclusions from very little evidence. For example, a man who is turned down by one woman after he asks for a date may draw the conclusion that all women will reject him and he will never get a date. The healthy thinker draws conclusions only after taking in a great deal of evidence.

## 3. Negative Mental Filter

This person filters out any bit of information that is positive or good. She just doesn't hear compliments or words of affirmation or praise. She hears only criticism. The healthy person hears both good and bad.

## 4. Disqualifying the Positive

This person hears the compliment but discounts it. He explains away words of affirmation or praise. For example, a person who is given a promotion may say, "I don't deserve this. They are just feeling sorry for me because I'm really such a loser." The healthy person receives compliments and praise, and uses them to validate his own self-esteem.

## 5. Jumping to Conclusions

This person believes she knows at all times, with 100 percent accuracy, what other people are thinking about her. The healthy person assumes she *isn't* a mind reader.

## 6. Magnification (Catastrophizing) or Minimization

This person exaggerates the importance of isolated events or encounters. He may magnify his own emotions, mistakes, or imperfections. He minimizes, however, any success he may have. A healthy-thinking person maximizes the good points and minimizes the failures.

## 7. Emotional Reasoning

This person sees an outcome as directly flowing from her emotions. For example, the person may feel hopeless about passing an exam, so she doesn't show up to take it. The healthy person separates current feelings from future events.

## 8. "Should" Statements

This person has a rigid set of internal rules about what should, must, ought to, can't, and has to be done. The healthy person knows and expresses the fact that there are very few hard-and-fast rules in life.

### 9. *Labeling and Mislabeling*

This person is likely to give himself or another person negative labels such as "stupid," "idiot," "imbecile," "loser," "jerk," or "pig." The healthy person avoids labels. (I like to remind people that God gave mankind the authority and responsibility of naming *animals,* not human beings.)

### 10. *Personalization*

This person blames himself for events over which he has no control or less control than he assumes. I've encountered a number of parents who blame themselves for their teenagers' experimentation with drugs. They become filled with guilt and self-judgment when the fact is, they need to hold the teenager accountable for *his* choices and behavior. The healthy person refuses to take responsibility or blame for someone else's freewill choices.[5]

## REFLECT AND REEXAMINE

I believe many people need to reflect upon several positions and opinions, and reexamine their beliefs about them:

### *"It's Best Kept a Secret"*

A person should keep very few things inside as secrets. The vast majority of secrets are negative. Unthinkable childhood traumas, such as incest and sexual abuse, can so mar the soul that bitterness and hatred smolder for decades, erupting many years later in the form of terrible nightmares, uncontrollable crying, an inability to function in the routines of life, depression, or some other negative behavior. Abusers often tell their victims, "Let's just keep this our little secret." Living with a horrendous secret only seems to work for so long before the weight of emotional baggage overcomes even the hardiest of souls.

## Love and Hate May Not Be Opposites

Some people have distortional thinking about love and hate. A high percentage of people I have met believe that love and hate are opposites. In my experience, people with extreme hate rarely have a capacity to show genuine love toward anyone, including themselves. Intense hate is usually born of rejection. Its true opposite is acceptance, which may or may not be the same as love. When a person begins to see that his hatred is rooted in rejection, he can then progress to forgiveness and a release of the toxic emotions he has been feeling.

## Pressure May Not Make for the Best Performance

People have said to me, "I work better under pressure."

Well, yes and no. A certain amount of pressure seems necessary to motivate some people to work, focus their energy, or prioritize their time. Rarely, however, do we do our best creative work or our best problem-solving and decision-making in an atmosphere of stress. Stress actually decreases a person's ability to cope with difficult circumstances.

## EXAMINE YOUR AUTOMATIC THOUGHTS

If I suspect that a patient has distortional thinking, I encourage that person to write in a journal all the ways in which her thinking may have become distorted or self-sabotaging. I ask her to write identifying statements for herself after monitoring the way she refers to herself and talks about herself.

My advice is this: Listen to yourself. Every time you hear yourself drawing a conclusion that may reflect any of Dr. Burns's ten thinking patterns—or anytime you hear yourself applying a label such as "stupid" to yourself—write it down.

Then I ask the person to go back through those journal entries and write next to each label or each possibility of distortional thinking a verse or short passage from the Bible that addresses that perception.

Next, I ask the person to confess to God that she has allowed herself to develop distortional thinking. She has bought into lies. I encourage the person to seek God's forgiveness and to ask God to set her free from the bondage that these lies have created in her soul. I encourage the person to ask God to heal the toxic emotions and distorted thinking that she has developed.

Finally, I advise the person to memorize the verses that she has written down in her journal. These are the foremost verses the person is likely to need, and to quote, in order to keep distortional thinking from continuing to take root.

Let me share some of the verses from the Bible that I believe have great transforming power when it comes to distortional thinking.

## TRANSFORMING TRUTHS

- I can do all things through Christ who strengthens me. (Phil. 4:13)

- Thanks be to God who always leads us in triumph in Christ. (2 Cor. 2:14)

- My God shall supply all your need according to His riches in glory by Christ Jesus. (Phil. 4:19)

- [Jesus said,] Do not intimidate anyone or accuse falsely, and be content with your wages. (Luke 3:14)

- Do not think it strange concerning the fiery trial which is to try you . . . but rejoice to the extent that you partake of Christ's sufferings, that when His glory is revealed, you may also be glad with exceeding joy. (1 Peter 4:12–13)

- Trust in the LORD with all your heart,
  And lean not on your own understanding;
  In all your ways acknowledge Him,
  And He shall direct your paths. (Prov. 3:5–6)

- Forgetting those things which are behind and reaching
  forward to those things which are ahead, I press toward the
  goal for the prize of the upward call of God in Christ Jesus.
  (Phil. 3:13–14)

- Do not be deceived, God is not mocked; for whatever a man
  sows, that he will also reap. (Gal. 6:7)

- He sent His word and healed them,
  And delivered them from their destructions. (Ps. 107:20)

- Bless the LORD, O my soul,
  And forget not all His benefits:
  Who forgives all your iniquities,
  Who heals all your diseases,
  Who redeems your life from destruction,
  Who crowns you with lovingkindness and tender mercies.
  (Ps. 103:2–4)

- Let us not grow weary while doing good, for in due season
  we shall reap if we do not lose heart. (Gal. 6:9)

I encourage you to purchase a Bible promises book that contains Scriptures regarding God's guarantees in the Bible, as well as a concordance that allows you to look up verses that are related to key concepts or words.

Every person has *some* degree of distortional thinking. The key to having a renewed mind—and to developing a mind that truly thinks as Christ Jesus thinks—is to confront distortional thinking continually with the truth of God. Seek to develop the ability to identify false thinking, recognize what kind of distortion is taking place, and then change the thought by replacing it with healthy, godly truth.

I have worked with countless people who have discovered that once they made a sincere effort to tackle their dysfunctional thought patterns, they had fewer bouts of depression, anxiety, anger, grief, shame, jealousy, and all other toxic emotions. It isn't difficult to replace lies with God's truth. It just takes intentional and consistent effort . . . it takes the time and energy to find statements of God's truth and apply them to life's lies. Jesus promised, "If you abide in My word, you are My disciples indeed. And you shall know the truth, and the truth shall make you free" (John 8:31–32).

## CHOOSE A NEW WAY OF THINKING

The apostle Paul challenged followers of Christ, "Do not be conformed to this world, but be transformed by the renewing of your mind, that you may prove what is that good and acceptable and perfect will of God" (Rom. 12:2). Part of experiencing a spiritual renewal in your mind is to make a conscious choice that you will change what you put into your mind, and therefore, change your thought patterns.

The Bible has this to say about the choices we make in our thought life: "Finally, brethren, whatever is true, whatever is honorable, whatever is right, whatever is pure, whatever is lovely, whatever is of good repute, if there is any excellence and if anything worthy of praise, let your mind dwell on these things" (Phil. 4:8 NASB).

Choose to think about those things that evoke positive emotions within you. Focus on them. Emphasize them. Reflect often on them. They are your best line of defense against toxic emotions.

John Hagee once said,

Watch your thoughts, for they will become your words. Choose your words, for they become actions. Understand your actions, for they become habits. Study your habits, for they will become your character. Develop your character, for it becomes your destiny.

# ─┤ 13 ├─

# THE CLEANSING POWER
# OF FORGIVENESS

Those who forgive are those who *choose* to forgive. There's nothing automatic, unintentional, or happenstance about forgiveness. It is a choice and an act of the will.

Those who choose to forgive are those who decide to give up resentment and the desire to punish. They have a willingness to relinquish all claims to exact a penalty for an offense. They actually cancel the debt they believe another person owes them.

Forgiveness enables a person to release buried anger, resentment, bitterness, shame, grief, regret, guilt, hate, and other toxic emotions that hide deep in the soul and make a person ill—both emotionally and physically. A permeating sense of peace that blankets a person's entire being commonly accompanies the cathartic act of true forgiveness.

Forgiveness releases layers of hurt and heals the raw, jagged edges of emotional pain. Saying "I forgive" is like taking an emotional shower—forgiveness cleanses and frees the entrapped soul.

Many times we have to take an initial step of forgiveness to *start* the forgiveness process. Sometimes we must repeat the act of forgiving each time a new set of painful memories comes to the surface.

One woman, who had divorced her abusive husband, said to me, "I know why Jesus said to forgive 70 times 7. I think I've forgiven my former husband 370 times by now. I just may need another 120 times of forgiveness before I get to the bottom of the forgiveness well!" (See Matt. 18:21–22.)

This woman had suffered from nightmares in which her former husband appeared in threatening postures and spoke demeaning words. She had mental flashbacks of his abusive behavior. On one hand she was sorry for the divorce, but on the other, she was greatly relieved. Divorce for her meant that she did not have to live in a daily state of confusion, frustration, humiliation, or the threat of physical harm.

Nevertheless, this woman also found that she wanted to see her husband punished for all the pain he had caused her. She wanted him to hurt as much as she had. She wanted him to love someone and then face that person's rejection so he would know the full anguish she had experienced. She knew that these thoughts and feelings of revenge were not compatible with forgiveness.

When she began to forgive, she embarked on emotional healing. She also told me, "My nightmares went away. My headaches went away. And my blood pressure dropped to normal levels."

It took nearly four years for this woman to feel as if she had *fully* forgiven her husband. She emerged from the forgiveness process stronger emotionally and physically—in fact, healthier than she had been during the seven years of their marriage and the first two years after the divorce. She had more energy, more strength, more general vitality, and more enthusiasm for the future. She told me she felt renewed hope and was making all sorts of plans that were positive and potentially fulfilling.

## HOW DO YOU DEFINE *FORGIVENESS*?

One of the reasons many people find it difficult to forgive is that they have a false understanding or a fuzzy concept of forgiveness. Let me be very clear about what I mean, and don't mean, when I use the word *forgiveness*.

Forgiveness is *not* based on finding some redeeming quality that makes a person *worth* forgiving. We can never base genuine forgiveness upon an individual's "good behavior" compensating for his previously hurtful behavior. Forgiveness is something that happens on the inside of you—it comes solely from your desire to forgive for the sake of forgiving.

Nobody who intentionally harms another person truly deserves forgiveness from the person he has hurt. Even so, it's far better to forgive and to live in the resulting emotional freedom and health than to suffer the consequences of failing to forgive.

Forgiveness does not require that a person minimize the validity of his pain, the amount of pain he suffered, or the importance of a painful experience. To forgive does *not* mean that a person is saying, "This didn't matter" or "This wasn't a huge wrong committed against me." Rather, it is saying, "I choose no longer to hold this feeling of unforgiveness toward the person who hurt me."

Forgiveness does not mean letting a person off the hook so that no justice is required. A forgiving person can still require a person to appear in court or face legal penalties for a crime committed against him. Forgiveness means putting another person squarely in the hands of God, and allowing God to work His justice in that person's life. It is trusting God to deal with the offending person, the hurtful situation, the horrible memories of terrible events. It is trusting God to heal the wound inside. In the end, God's justice—coupled with His mercy, love, and desire to redeem and forgive—will always be far superior to man's.

Some contend that emotional wounds heal over time. I have rarely seen that to be the case. Memories may fade slightly over time. People may mature and change over time. But there's nothing about time that causes a painful toxic emotion automatically to dissipate. Extremely painful events in childhood can hurt just as much seventy or eighty years later.

We may brush off minor hurts, superficial offenses, and irritating trespasses in seconds or minutes. But forgiving deep emotional wounds and seriously damaging offenses is nearly always a process. Often it takes both time and intentional effort to forgive.

We must never lose sight of the fact that forgiveness is a matter of the will.

WE MUST NEVER LOSE SIGHT OF THE FACT THAT
FORGIVENESS IS A MATTER OF THE WILL.

Finally, forgiveness is an act of strength. Some people see forgiveness as a flaw in a weak person. Nothing could be farther from the truth. It takes little inner fortitude to harbor anger, resentment, or hate. It takes a great deal of courage to lay down one's anger and seek to walk away in peace. Some of the people considered the strongest have voiced the need to forgive. Mahatma Gandhi once said, "The weak can never forgive. Forgiveness is the attribute of the strong."

## IT TAKES TWO TO RECONCILE

It takes only one person to forgive. It takes two to reconcile. You can forgive a person if he doesn't forgive you, but reconciliation always requires the wills of both parties involved. That's an important distinction to make.

One of the most powerful modern-day stories of forgiveness is one I saw several years ago on *Larry King Live*. Jim Bakker and his former wife, Tammy Faye Messner, appeared on the program together to tell how they had forgiven each other, themselves, and everyone else surrounding their downfall from Christian television in the 1980s owing to major accusations of financial fraud and an illicit sexual affair.

Both Jim and Tammy told stories of deep hurts and forgiveness. Both had felt betrayed by a minister for the loss of their ministry, but both had been able to forgive this man. Tammy had forgiven Jim for his adulterous sexual encounter. Jim had forgiven his wife for divorcing him and marrying his best friend while he was incarcerated.

Regarding Jim's affair, Tammy said, "Forgiveness is a choice. Our whole lives are made up of choices. I could have chosen to be bitter and hate him, or I could have chosen to forgive. It was very hard for me to forgive him. It was very hard, but, I was able to forgive him and understand what happened and go on."

Regarding Tammy's remarriage and those who had attacked his ministry, Jim said, "The Bible is so clear, and this is what I studied in prison. When I began to study the words of Jesus Christ, I learned that He said if you don't forgive from the heart—forgiving everyone—you will not be forgiven. Christ said, 'Blessed are the merciful for they shall obtain mercy.' I needed mercy, I needed forgiveness, so I wanted to give out to others what I myself needed."[1]

You may forgive but find the other person unwilling to reconcile. If that happens, know that you have done your part. Leave behind the toxic emotions between you and that person. Trust God to do His work in the other person's life, in His timing, and using His methods.

Also recognize that there are some situations in which reconciliation may not be advisable, such as in cases of domestic abuse, stalking, violent behavior, or sexual abuse of a child. If that is the case, don't beat up yourself emotionally for a failure to reconcile. God requires forgiveness of you, not a reuniting with a person who has hurt you or who exhibits ongoing destructive behavior.

## FORGIVENESS OPENS THE DOOR TO LOVE

Some contend that forgiveness flows, almost automatically it seems, from a loving heart. The opposite is true. Forgiveness leads to an ability to love. It's virtually impossible to love a person against whom you are holding a grudge, with whom you have had a painful encounter, or from whom you have experienced rejection or emotional pain. Love doesn't come first. Forgiveness does.

A psychiatrist named George Ritchie has written about World War II death-camp survivors. Here is what he wrote about a man named Wild Bill:

[Wild Bill] was one of the inmates of the concentration camp, but obviously he hadn't been there long. His posture was erect, his eyes bright, his energy indefatigable. Since he was fluent in English, French, German, and Russian, as well as Polish, he became a kind of unofficial camp translator.

Though Wild Bill worked fifteen and sixteen hours a day, he showed no signs of weariness. While the rest of us were drooping with fatigue, he seemed to gain strength.

I was astonished to learn when Wild Bill's own papers came before us one day, he had been in Wuppertal since 1939! For six years he had lived on the same starvation diet, slept in the same airless and disease-ridden barracks as everyone else, but without the least physical or mental deterioration.

Wild Bill was our greatest asset, reasoning with the different groups, counseling forgiveness.

"It's not easy for some of them to forgive," I commented to him one day. "So many of them have lost members of their families."

"We lived in the Jewish section of Warsaw," he began slowly, the first words I had heard him speak about himself, "my wife, our two daughters, and our three little boys. When the Germans reached our street they lined everyone against the wall and opened up with machine guns. I begged to be allowed to die with my family, but because I spoke German they put me in a work group.

"I had to decide right then," he continued, "whether to let myself hate the soldiers who had done this. It was an easy decision, really. I was a lawyer. In my practice I had seen too often what hate could do to people's minds and bodies. Hate had just killed the six people who mattered most to me in the world. I decided then that I would spend the rest of my life—whether it was a few days or many years—loving every person I came in contact with."

That was the power that had kept a man well in the face of every privation.[2]

The healthiest people among us seem to be those generous souls who laugh easily, forget unpleasant events quickly, and are quick to forgive even the gravest offenses. This kind of childlikeness keeps a person unencumbered emotionally and spiritually, and in the end, unencumbered physically. It is no mystery to me as a physician that the Bible teaches us to become "as little children" in our relationship with God and in our ability to forgive, believe, and express our faith (Matt. 18:3).

Only genuine forgiveness can quench the hot coals of toxic emotions. Only genuine forgiveness can free a person to live free of the searing, scarring remnants of deep inner hurt.

## THE HEALTH BENEFITS OF FORGIVENESS

A scientific project conducted at the University of Wisconsin was simply called "The Forgiveness Study." The study demonstrated that learning to forgive may help prevent heart disease in middle-aged subjects. The incidence of heart disease was higher in those who admitted they could not forgive. The risk of heart disease was much lower in those who reported an ability to forgive easily. These researchers concluded that a failure to forgive is a greater predictor of physical health problems than hostility.[3]

Dr. Fred Luskin, whom I mentioned earlier, was the director of the Stanford Forgiveness Project at Stanford University. Part of his work involved projects he labeled HOPE—Healing Our Past Experiences. In one of these projects Luskin worked with adults between the ages of twenty-five and fifty who had been hurt emotionally and could not forgive. Some of these adults had spouses who had cheated on them. Others were married to spouses with alcohol or drug problems. Still others felt abandoned by their best friends.

The ongoing results of this project are still being published, but one of the conclusions Luskin and his associates drew is this: the person who is taught to forgive a particular individual or offense becomes much more forgiving in a broader, more generalized sense. Those who develop an ability to forgive have greater control over their emotions and they are significantly less angry, less upset, and feel less hurt when compared to those who receive no training in how to forgive or have no ability to forgive.

In these adults who learn to forgive, Luskin found a significant decrease in the number of physical complaints.

One of Luskin's studies involved five women from North Ireland. Four of the women had lost sons to political violence. As the women learned how to forgive, they found they were able to display increased forgiveness toward those who had killed their sons. The women reported that they felt significantly more optimistic, and their depression scores also improved.[4]

In a related study, levels of emotional hurt plummeted nearly 40 percent in one week of forgiveness training, and depression declined significantly as well. Participants reported a statistically significant increase in their feelings of physical vitality and general well-being, and 35 percent of the people in the study said they felt "less distress."[5]

## THE CONSEQUENCES OF FAILING TO FORGIVE

If you choose not to forgive someone, I guarantee that your toxic, deadly emotions of resentment and hatred will continue to poison your system in ways that are just as dangerous as your taking in a literal poison. Not only will your body suffer, but your mind, spirit, and your general emotional well-being will suffer.

In failing to forgive, you really are hurting only yourself. Unforgiveness rarely hurts the person who offended you. Most of the people you are unwilling to forgive don't even realize you are upset with them. Many people are so rude or uncaring that they don't know when they offend others.

MOST OF THE PEOPLE YOU ARE UNWILLING TO FORGIVE DON'T EVEN REALIZE YOU ARE UPSET WITH THEM.

I was discussing this recently with a friend and she told me that she had felt for years that a particular person at her church didn't like her. She admitted she had harbored resentful feelings against that person. She told me that she had approached this woman and another person to whom she was talking. The woman had failed to acknowledge her presence, although Jane had been sure the woman had seen her as she approached them. Furthermore, she thought she heard her name mentioned in the conversation these two women were having, which had led her to conclude they were gossiping about her.

Years later, Jane learned that the other person in the conversation had been pouring out a personal problem to the woman Jane thought had slighted her. The personal problem involved a woman named Jane! My friend Jane said she suddenly realized in a moment's time that these two women had been so deep in conversation that they hadn't been aware she was standing so close to them. She also realized that had they acknowledged her, she may have interrupted a much-needed counseling session there in the lobby of her church.

She said, "I harbored resentment and suspicion in my heart for years and it was totally unfounded. Through that I learned I'm better off to forgive and let some things go, especially if there's any doubt that I may have misinterpreted the behavior of another person."

Misperceptions are often involved in cases of feeling slighted, misunderstood, or rejected.

## FORGIVENESS IS A PROCESS

We often need to express and feel forgiveness in a step-by-step progression. I see the process as having these stages:

### Admit You Have Been Wounded

Before you can forgive, you need to openly admit to yourself that events, words, situations, or attitudes have hurt or wounded you emotionally and spiritually—in your past or your current life. Admit that the offense has occurred, no matter how slight you think it is.

Many times people say, "I know this shouldn't bother me" or "People tell me I should have expected this" or "I'm probably making a bigger deal of this than I should." Don't dismiss, deny, or diminish the hurt you have felt. Acknowledge that what happened to you brought you emotional pain.

People have told me, "Oh, I forgave the person"—and then they will proceed to tell me things that make it very clear they haven't truly forgiven. They may have said the words "I forgive you," but they never truly released the offenders from their hearts.

I recently heard about a woman who is now nearly sixty years old whose uncle sexually abused her for a number of years. Her uncle had come to her when she was fifteen and said, "Your aunt knows what has happened. I'll never try to have sex with you again. Please forgive me."

As a wounded and scarred—not to mention intimidated and scared—fifteen-year-old, this young woman said, "I forgive you."

Nearly forty years later, suffering from severe insomnia and a greatly suppressed immune system that seemed to make her vulnerable to every virus or bacteria that came along, she had to admit, "I forgave him with words from my mouth. I may even have forgiven him in my head. But I have never truly forgiven him in my heart."

*Accept God's Forgiveness in Your Life*

According to the Bible, the only way a person can fully and deeply forgive another person is to know first that God has forgiven him. God's forgiveness of us forms the basis for our ability to forgive others. Look at Jesus' words:

- [Pray,] Forgive us our debts, as we forgive our debtors. (Matt. 6:12)

- If you forgive men their trespasses, your heavenly Father will also forgive you. But if you do not forgive men their trespasses, neither will your Father forgive your trespasses. (Matt. 6:14–15)

- Judge not, and you shall not be judged. Condemn not, and you shall not be condemned. Forgive, and you will be forgiven. (Luke 6:37)

If you believe you had any part whatsoever in the wrong committed against you, confess that to God and receive His forgiveness. And then, forgive yourself. Accept the fact that God's forgiveness is complete. In fact, the Bible tells us that what God forgives, God forgets (see Ps. 103:12).

If you believe you had absolutely no part whatsoever in the wrong committed against you, you will still be wise to ask God to forgive you for harboring any unforgiveness against the person. Ask God to heal you of the painful memories you have of the event or circumstances in which you were hurt.

### Openly Release the Offender to God's Hands

Some time ago I talked with a person who told me that when he counsels people who need to forgive, he hands them a small rubbery toy. He tells them to hold on to that toy with all their strength, using both hands. And then he says, "Now, if you are ready to forgive, I want to lead you in a prayer. I want you to see the person you are forgiving as being like that little rubber toy you are squeezing so hard. That's the way unforgiveness works in your soul. You are holding on to this person and the time has come to release him. As we pray, I want you to let go of this person and place him in the hands of God. Let go of the toy. And then, turn your palms up and receive God's love. Lay your hands over your heart."

I asked, "What happens when you do this?"

He said, "At times, the person can hardly let go. He thinks it will be easy, but it is very difficult. Sometimes when the person does let go, he begins to sob—very often for quite a while. And it's only after all the tears are out that a person finds he can truly receive God's love in his own heart. Many people aren't prepared for forgiveness to be so emotional."

"Is it always this way?" I asked.

He replied, "Well, unforgiveness is an emotion. So there's always emotion involved if the forgiveness is genuine. Some people are less demonstrative in their emotions than others, but forgiveness is emotional. It can't help but be—it's the emotions that are being healed."

*Ask God to Help You*

Ask God to help you to forgive the person who has offended you. He knows far more about forgiveness than any human being! Trust Him to impart to you the ability to forgive fully and freely.

*Voice Your Forgiveness*

Focus on the name of a person who has hurt you, harshly judged you, falsely labeled you, or in any way brought you feelings of emotional pain or distress. Speak that person's name in the blank provided in the following prayer:

Heavenly Father, I choose today to forgive _____ _____ of any offense committed against me, whether knowingly or unknowingly. I release to You all of the memories and toxic emotions of unforgiveness that may be buried in my heart. I declare before You right now that this event, situation, or circumstance of offense against me is now dead forever. Heal me, Father. Help me to move forward in the freedom and strength of forgiveness.

In my experience of having patients pray this prayer, I have found that some people begin to experience a flood of memories. They think they are forgiving just one offense, but suddenly five new offenses take its place. It's a little like the cork being popped from a champagne bottle.

I encourage the person, as he recalls each new offense, to repeat the forgiveness prayer. At times, I've had a person repeat this prayer a dozen times or more. Let me assure you, the end result has been far greater joy and release than the person ever thought would happen when the prayer time began!

*Consider Whether You Need to Ask or Grant Forgiveness to the Offending Person*

There may be times when your process of forgiveness is complete only when you ask another person to forgive you. Sometimes you need to go to a person who has asked for your forgiveness—and from whom you have withheld it—and grant the forgiveness requested. Forgiveness is the foremost gift we can give to another person.

## PARTIAL VS. FULL FORGIVENESS

Superficial or partial forgiveness brings no real emotional cleansing. When a person partially forgives another, he may experience a decrease in negative feelings, but he gains no genuine emotional freedom or peace in his heart. Partial forgiveness tends to happen in the head. People forgive because they think it's a good idea or the right thing to do. They mouth the words and think they have forgiven, but deep inside, memories of the offense still trigger pangs of pain and resentful feelings.

A person who only partially forgives experiences only a partial reconciliation with the one who offended him. Attempts to restore friendship fail. Hurtful memories continue to rise up. He feels little warmth or affection toward the person who wounded him.

Full forgiveness, in contrast, allows a total release of all negative feelings once directed toward the offender. This type of forgiveness is cleansing and cathartic.

If you are still working at forgiveness, and you sincerely desire to experience full forgiveness and a cathartic cleansing, be encouraged that release *will come* if you continue to ask God to help you forgive.

## FORGIVING YOURSELF

Perhaps the most difficult act of forgiveness is forgiving ourselves. To be truly cleansed and to move forward into emotional well-being, we must take a look at our own lives, and in those areas where we see we have failed, to ask for God's forgiveness.

Once we have asked God for forgiveness, we need to truly believe that God has forgiven us. The Bible promises, "If we confess our sins, He is faithful and just to forgive us our sins and to cleanse us from all unrighteousness" (1 John 1:9).

Then we need to forgive ourselves. Failing to do this can result in shame, remorse, guilt, and regret.

Some people find it very difficult to forgive themselves for the abuse they have showered on spouses or children, for extramarital affairs they have had, for abortions, drug or alcohol abuse, or for squandering the family's money on gambling.

The apostle Paul wrote these words of encouragement: "One thing I do, forgetting those things which are behind and reaching forward to those things which are ahead, I press toward the goal for the prize of the upward call of God in Christ Jesus" (Phil. 3:13–14).

It isn't enough that a person simply says, "Oh well, that was in the past. I'll forget that and go forward." To do that is to dismiss the vitally important step of forgiveness. Confession of sin and experiencing God's forgiveness are vital in being able truly to forget the past.

At the same time, once we have confessed our sins to God and received His forgiveness, we should press toward the goal that lies ahead. This pressing on includes an active, intentional act of goal-setting and of looking to the future with hope, fully believing, "I can do all things through Christ who strengthens me" (Phil. 4:13).

You may very well discover that once you have worked through your own process of forgiveness, you will one day look back and realize that what happened to you has been turned into a blessing in your life, not the grievance and scar you had initially thought it to be.

Genuine forgiveness produces healing emotions—love, deep peace of mind and heart, and genuine joy. I encourage you to begin embracing these wonderful emotions that God intended for your wholeness.

## LIVING IN A STATE OF FORGIVENESS

Choose to live in a state of forgiveness. The only way to do that is to ask God's forgiveness daily and to forgive daily all those who may have harmed, ridiculed, persecuted, rejected, criticized, or maligned you, or who otherwise trespassed on your peace of mind and your personal faith.

If you are struggling with forgiveness, I encourage you to read and study all the Bible has to say about it. Use a concordance to find the many references. The Bible has a number of stories and teachings about forgiveness.

- Joseph's story is a wonderful account of a young man who experienced repeated injustices; but in the end, he came to believe that all of the injustices served God's ultimately positive purposes in his life and in the lives of his family members. (See Gen. 37–45.)

- The parable of the prodigal son is a story of a father's generous forgiveness. (See Luke 15:11–32.)

- The parable of a servant who owed an enormous debt is a story about our need to forgive. (See Matt. 18:23–35.)

Ongoing forgiveness keeps toxic, deadly emotions from building up. Daily forgiveness is my foremost prescription for a person's total mental, emotional, spiritual, and physical health.

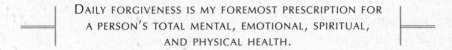

DAILY FORGIVENESS IS MY FOREMOST PRESCRIPTION FOR A PERSON'S TOTAL MENTAL, EMOTIONAL, SPIRITUAL, AND PHYSICAL HEALTH.

A great Bible passage to commit to memory is this one: "Let all bitterness, wrath, anger, clamor, and evil speaking be put away from you, with all malice. And be kind to one another, tenderhearted, forgiving one another, even as God in Christ forgave you" (Eph. 4:31–32).

# 14

# THE THERAPEUTIC VALUE OF JOY

Joy is a deeply personal emotion. No one can truly tell if another person is joyful on the inside. One of the external manifestations of joy, however, is nearly always a quickness to smile and an ability to laugh deeply.

Several years ago I treated a woman named Samantha. Sammi, as her friends and I came to call her, had been spending many hours each day in bed, suffering from severe fibromyalgia, chronic fatigue, high blood pressure, and arthritis. I recognized in the course of my history-taking that Sammi was also in serious emotional depression. I addressed her depression even as we gave her medications to help with the symptoms of her physical ailments.

As the weeks passed, Sammi began to have some good days. Her symptoms started to dissipate in a way that was nearly parallel to the emotional therapy she was receiving and the lifting of her depression. Before long, Sammi was having more good days than bad. Once in a while, however, she would plummet into the depths of despair. I met with her on one of those occasions and I immediately reached for my prescription pad and wrote this out: *Have at least ten belly laughs a day.*

She seemed very surprised when I handed the prescription to her. I said, "Sammi, how long has it been since you had a really good belly laugh—the kind that made you want to roll on the floor with your eyes watering and your sides splitting?"

She said, "I don't know if I've ever laughed like that."

I said, "Well, laughter is your prescription. Go out and buy yourself the funniest joke book you can find. Rent or buy some movies and old television comedies. Then sit down and read or watch yourself into laughter. Do that every time a dark cloud looms on the horizon of your soul, or anytime you find that your body seems to be suddenly gripped by pain. I want you to laugh away that gloom and that pain!"

The next time I met Sammi, her countenance was completely different. She walked into the waiting room as if she owned the place, grabbed my hand, and gave me such a big bear hug I nearly lost my breath. Everything about her seemed to be transformed: her voice, her facial expressions, her walk. With a twinkle in her eyes and a wide smile she declared to everybody within hearing range, "Dr. Colbert, I've learned how to laugh! I've never felt so good in my entire life!"

The Bible says, "A merry heart does good, like medicine" (Prov. 17:22). In my practice of prescribing laughter, I've seen the truth of that verse borne out many times.

## LAUGHTER IS GOOD MEDICINE

Loma Linda University Medical Center's Dr. Lee Berk has written about the health and healing benefits of laughter. He concluded that laughter boosts the immune system and reduces dangerous stress hormones in the body. In one study involving sixteen men who watched a funny video, levels of the stress hormone cortisol fell 39 percent after a good belly laugh. Adrenaline (epinephrine) levels fell 70 percent, while levels of the feel-good hormone endorphin rose 27 percent. Not only that, but growth hormone (the "youth hormone") levels skyrocketed 87 percent.[1]

Berk's findings about cortisol are especially important. Cortisol is the dangerous stress hormone that, once elevated for extended periods of time, can act like acid in the body. It especially affects the brain, eventually causing memory loss. It is hard to lower cortisol medically once its level rises. Laughter truly is a good prescription!

Berk and others have shown that laughter can lower blood pressure. In 2000, a team of researchers at the University of Maryland reported that individuals who used humor in their speech patterns often were less likely to suffer a heart attack than those who didn't. Still other researchers have found that people with a good sense of humor experience overall "less stress and better health."[2]

In his research, Berk reported that laughter helps the immune system in very specific ways:

- It increases immunoglobulin A, which helps protect against respiratory tract infections.

- It increases gamma interferon—the immune system's frontline defense against viruses.

- It increases B cells that produce antibodies directly against harmful bacteria.

- It increases complement 2, a combination of proteins that acts as a catalyst in antibody reactions.[3]

Norman Cousins, journalist and former editor of the *Saturday Review*, developed an extremely painful disease of the connective tissue called ankylosing spondylitis. The disease caused such extreme pain that he could barely move his joints. Playing tennis, traveling, or just participating in day-to-day activities he once enjoyed suddenly became excruciatingly painful.

Cousins refused to accept his doctor's gloomy prognosis. With his body racked with pain, he recalled an article he had read that negative emotions might predispose a person to certain diseases, this particular disease among them. He began to wonder if negative emotions were linked to his ailment and to question whether positive emotions might work in an opposite manner to bring healing. He figured a personal experiment was in order. He began watching funny movies in order to make himself laugh to see if laughter influenced his level of pain. The Marx Brothers and *Candid Camera* became his favorite therapy, in addition to enjoying regular belly laughs through telling jokes and playing practical jokes on other people. He even had nurses read humorous stories to him.

Over time, he noticed that laughing before going to bed helped him sleep. In fact, ten minutes of genuine belly laughter had something of an anesthetic affect, providing him at least two hours of pain-free sleep. When the pain-killing effect of laughter began to wear off, Cousins switched on another funny movie. After he had laughed at least ten minutes, he found he could go back to sleep for another two-hour interval.

As the laughter therapy continued, Cousins noticed something else begin to happen. He was getting well! The inflammation in his body, measured according to his sed rate (a measure of inflammation), started to decrease after a session of laughter. Over time, the sed rate dropped to normal. Cousins got well. The *New England Journal of Medicine* documented the remarkable story of his use of laughter in December 1976.[4] The study birthed a book, titled *Anatomy of an Illness,* published in 1979.

The healing power of laughter became a life passion for Cousins, who worked with Loma Linda University in conducting research on how laughter affects stress hormones and the immune system. Cousins spent the final twelve years of his life at UCLA Medical School, where he worked as an adjunct professor and set up a humor task force to conduct clinical research on laughter. This research has now been ongoing for twenty years at the UCLA Norman Cousins Center for Psychoneuroimmunology, which is presently conducting research under the umbrella title of "Rx Laughter Study."

In this study, medical personnel are showing extremely ill children funny videos, cartoons, television shows, and films to see how laughter impacts their immune systems. Researchers are finding that children are healing faster and with less pain. One of the professors involved has said, "Laughter seems to induce a relaxation response in the autonomic nervous system . . . this would be useful in helping children who are undergoing painful procedures or who suffer from pain expectation anxiety."[5]

## MORE EXPERIENCES AND ASPECTS
## OF HEALTHY HUMOR

### An Epidemic of Laughter

I was fascinated to learn of a recorded instance of a "laughter epidemic" in Africa. It occurred in 1963 and the *Central African Journal of Medicine* documented it.

The laughter began at a Catholic girls' school in Bukoba, Tanganyika, when two girls began to giggle. Soon the whole class was laughing, including the teachers. Very quickly, the whole school was laughing. Laughter spread to mothers and fathers, and before long the entire village was overcome. The laughter spread to a number of nearby communities, and it continued for a full two weeks. This was the kind of laughter that was deep, hearty, and couldn't seem to be stopped.

Have you ever found yourself laughing more, the more you tried not to laugh? This is the kind of laughter that occurred in Bukoba. The people in this area laughed so intensely that tears flowed and some had to be treated for exhaustion. In all, more than a thousand people were affected by this laughter epidemic, the longest such epidemic on record.[6]

### As Good As Exercise?

One researcher has concluded that laughter's effect in the body is similar to a good aerobic exercise. Dr. William Fry Jr. has researched the potential therapeutic properties of laughter and humor for more than thirty years. He contends that laughter ventilates the lungs and leaves the muscles, nerves, and heart warm and relaxed—the very same benefits of aerobic exercise.[7] Cousins had noted in his experience this effect: He said that laughter was like "internal jogging."[8] Others have likened the effects of laughter to those of a deep massage.

As with aerobic exercise, laughter temporarily speeds up the heart rate, increases blood pressure and breathing, expands circulation, and enhances the flow of oxygen in and out of the body.

A good belly laugh also exercises the upper torso, lungs, and heart, as well as the shoulders, arms, abdomen, diaphragm, and legs. Laughing one hundred to two hundred times a day is equal to ten minutes of rowing or jogging. Some researchers contend that twenty seconds of belly laughter is equivalent to three minutes of working out on a rowing machine.[9] In my opinion, bring on the laughter!

### Helpful to the Brain

Humor also is helpful to the brain. It allows a person to use both sides of his brain simultaneously. When a person tells a joke, the left side of the brain is active. When a person "gets" a joke and starts laughing, the right side comes into play.

Some research has shown that people are more creative in problem-solving after they perceive something as humorous. Other studies suggest that laughter helps increase the flexibility and creativity of thought.

## START WITH A SMILE

Laughter is infectious. In most cases, it is a spontaneous response. Few people can force themselves to begin a belly laugh. How, then, can a person learn to laugh? By choosing to smile.

The average adult laughs twenty-five times a day and the average child four hundred times a day, according to humor expert Patty Wooten. One of the first expressions an infant makes is a smile, and this occurs sometimes as early as at six weeks of age. Even children born blind or deaf have an intuitive "smile response" when they feel pleasure.[10] Smiles are built into you—it's up to you to choose to express them!

## SMILES ARE BUILT INTO YOU—IT'S UP TO YOU TO CHOOSE TO EXPRESS THEM!

So . . . choose to smile.

- Smile at other people. Smiling is nearly a universal language. A smile is an act of friendship across virtually all races, cultures, languages, and nations.

- Smile at things that seem to be absurdities, flaws, or anomalies in life.

- Smile at the sunshine or beauty of nature. Smile at the opportunity to run through the rain or the sprinklers.

- Smile at the children you see playing in the park.

- Smile at the memory of a happy moment or time spent in a pleasant place.

Laughter comes on the heels of smiling. While smiling may not be quite as therapeutic as laughing, smiling does have physical benefits in the body. Facial expressions are connected neurologically to emotional states. Not only do laughter and smiling *reflect* an inner emotional state, but these expressions can *trigger* an emotional state. A smile on the face can cause a response in the heart.[11]

In one study I found particularly interesting, researchers asked participants to contort their faces to form an expression of anger. The researchers did not say to the participants, "Look angry." Instead, they told them to move their eyebrows close together, a facial expression that often accompanies anger. When they asked the participants later how they felt after doing this, the vast majority of them said they felt "angry."

The researchers measured the heart rate, muscle activity, and finger temperatures of those they asked to twist their faces into various emotional poses. The results showed that facial expressions can stimulate specific physiological changes in the body.[12]

What can we conclude? Even if you don't feel like smiling, smile! The more you *choose* to smile, the more you will feel like smiling. And in the end, the better you'll feel overall, both emotionally and physically.

## Two Kinds of Smiles

Researchers have found that there are two types of smiles. One type is disingenuous or inauthentic. This is the fake smile that we plaster on our faces when someone says, "Say 'cheese.'" The second is the genuine article, called the "Duchenne smile" after Guillaume Duchenne, who first wrote about this type of smile. He described this smile as causing the skin around the corners of the eyes to crinkle and the corners of the mouth to turn up. The muscles that make this smile possible—the *orbicularis oculi* and the *zygomaticus*—are more difficult to control voluntarily than the muscles needed to generate a fake smile.[13]

Smile researchers Dacher Keltner and LeeAnne Harker studied the class photos from a 1960 yearbook at Mills College. Of the 141 photos in the book, all but three were of smiling women, and half of those smiling were Duchenne smilers.

The researchers contacted the female smilers at the ages of twenty-seven, forty-three, and fifty-two and questioned them about their happiness and life satisfaction in marriage. The women with Duchenne smiles were more likely to be married and to have stayed married, and to experience more personal well-being than the "phony smilers" or "no smilers."[14]

I recently came across a brief poetic essay a nurse named Leslie Gibson wrote at the Morton Plant Hospital. I like its message.

### A SMILE

A smile costs nothing, but gives much. It enriches those who give it. It takes but a moment, but the memory of it sometimes lasts forever.

None is so rich or mighty that he can get along without it, and none is so poor but that he cannot be made richer by it.

A smile creates happiness in the home, promotes good will in business, and is the cornerstone of friendship. It can perk up the weary, bring cheer to the discouraged, sunshine to the sad, and is nature's best antidote for trouble.

Yet, it cannot be bought, begged, borrowed, or stolen, for it is something that is of no value to anyone until it is given away.

When people are too tired to give you a smile, give them one of yours. No one needs a smile so much as he who has none to give.[15]

## THE PURSUIT OF JOY

Happiness and joy are not the same. Happiness is a feeling of pleasure, contentment, or a sense of well-being that comes from the outer environment or event that a person is experiencing. It is temporary and dependent upon external factors—including what others say and do.

Joy, in contrast, is abiding or enduring. It comes from a feeling of contentment deep inside a person. It is not dependent on external factors, but on an inner sense of value, purpose, fulfillment, or satisfaction.

Pleasure that produces happiness tends to come through the five senses; for example, eating a delicious chocolate dessert, hearing a beautiful piece of music, or snuggling under a warm, soft blanket. Happiness comes from pleasure-producing perceptions one enjoys while attending an exciting football game, receiving a relaxing massage, hearing a compliment, receiving a gift, finding the perfect item on sale, visiting an amusement park, and so forth.

Happiness-producing pleasures can induce an addiction, and in that regard a person needs to be careful. If drinking alcohol gives a person a sense of pleasure, then overdrinking alcohol can lead to alcoholism. The same for drugs: if taking drugs or even certain prescription medicine gives a person pleasure, a person may be induced to take more drugs or to "overtake" a prescription. Sex, gambling, eating—almost anything that triggers a pleasure response in a person can become addictive.

If your goal is to find happiness through pleasures that are bound to the five senses, you will never be fully satisfied. You will always be looking for more.

## The Happiness Trap

There's a trap associated with happiness. Happiness sometimes comes when a person takes the path of least resistance. For example, a person may desire to be a teacher. The path to becoming a teacher requires academic training and student-teaching hours that are long and sometimes difficult. In light of these facts, a person studying to be a teacher may opt for the happiness of an easier career path. In the end, however, the person who trades in a long-term goal on short-term ease or happiness tends to end up in a position he hates. Stick with the tougher, longer, harder pursuit that is truly rooted in your talents and desires. In the end, you'll find the joy you desired.

Marriage is another example. Sometimes people opt for the quick affair, thinking happiness lies in experiencing pleasure wherever they can find it. Marriage is tough work, but in the long run, those who are married find greater joy and satisfaction in life than those who aren't.[16] Stick with the relationship that has the greater potential for long-term joy.

Sometimes a person pursues a career thinking that the related money or prestige will bring him joy. That's nearly always the wrong motivation. And it isn't true. The average income for Americans has risen significantly over the past thirty years, yet the percentage of people rating themselves as happy has steadily declined. During the past thirty years, the number of those who say they are happy has fallen from 36 to 29 percent.[17]

A new home, car, piece of jewelry, or outfit may give a person a temporary feeling of happiness, but these things don't produce long-lasting joy.

I've been with a number of people as they lay on their deathbeds, and I've never heard one of those people say he wished he had worked longer hours and made more money. Instead, I have heard my patients, often with tears in their eyes, say they wish they had spent more time with their families.

A lawyer is the highest-paid professional in the United States. A recent poll, however, stated that a whopping 52 percent of practicing attorneys describe themselves as "dissatisfied."[18] Lawyers are also at much greater risk than the general population for developing depression—they suffer depression at a rate 3.6 times higher than the general employed population, and they suffer from alcoholism and illegal drug use at a far higher rate than other professionals.[19] Not only are they generally unhappy, but unhealthy as well.

Seek out what you believe will really yield long-lasting, abiding *joy*.

## JOY IS A CHOICE

Joy does not flow from situations. It flows from your will and your emotions deep within. You can choose to be joyful, or you can choose to be miserable. Nobody can make these inner choices for you.

If you realize that you are not a frequent smiler or laugher, or that you are not a joyful person, you may want to ask yourself, "Why not?"

Some people lose their joy as a consequence of the homes in which they grew up. It's easy to have joy snuffed out in an atmosphere where rules are overly strict, parents don't show enough affection, or no one ever voices the words "I love you."

Some people lose their joy because they allow themselves to become overbooked with too many responsibilities and obligations, deadlines that are too tight, or workloads that are too heavy. Exhaustion, burnout, and disappointment can all sap a person's joy.

Some people lose their joy because they stop setting goals or making plans. I recently heard about two ninety-year-old men who were planning a cross-country trip together, taking a series of buses, boats, and trains. One of the men told me, "Even if we never do this trip, we are having a lot of fun thinking about it and planning it out. Every day we get together with our maps and a pile of brochures. We imagine ourselves in various places doing various things—some of which I can't tell you, son." The man who was talking to me winked. I have no idea where these men are thinking of going or what they are planning to do, but I know this: they are having a great time just contemplating their trip. Every day is a day for joy!

Some people allow a relationship problem to rob them of joy. Just as a fever is a sign of infection in the body, so the absence of laughter, humor, or a smile may be an indication or sign that something is seriously wrong in a relationship. If you have lost the laughter in your marriage, there's a good chance your marriage won't last long. Find something the two of you can chuckle about.

## LEARNING TO LIGHTEN UP

Has anyone ever told you to "lighten up"? Heeding their advice may be to your physical, mental, and emotional benefit! It is to every person's benefit if he can learn to laugh at his own foibles and mistakes.

Sigmund Freud identified the three parts of the emotional mind as the "parent," "adult," and "child." He noted that the child part of the mind is completely unconscious, while the parent part of the mind is completely conscious. The adult mind is partly unconscious, partly conscious. He concluded that too many people have locked away the child part of their emotional mind—sadly so, because when the parent or adult mind rules the emotions, life tends to be drained of joy, fun, or zest.

Are you aware that the word *silly* comes from the Greek word *selig,* which means *blessed*? Indeed, there's something very blessed in being silly, playful, and having the heart of a child.

### Develop a Sense of Play

See what you do as play, not work. Grown-ups can get preoccupied with making money, paying bills, doing chores, meeting challenges, shouldering responsibilities. Children, however, see life as a series of experiences that are enjoyable learning activities or simply fun things to do. A child can play "store" and handle play money . . . work at playing "kitchen" or "carpenter" . . . struggle to learn to use a jump rope or play jacks . . . and exert great effort in taking food and water out to the family dog. And they do so smiling, laughing, and relaxing. They can run around a park for hours and never once think of it as the work of exercise.

I strongly encourage you to take time regularly to play games with a child. Learn to see the world as the child does: as a great place to explore, as being filled with unusual and interesting things and people, as being one continual challenge to overcome.

I have cancer patients who admit to me that they haven't laughed for *years.* My first piece of advice to them is to find a child or pet to play with, and relearn how to see the humor in life. See the antics of the child as being humorous; become amused at the things that amuse the child; smile at the things the child smiles at.

### Delight in Humorous Stories

I mentioned Victor Frankl in a previous chapter. Frankl was a psychiatrist and survivor of the Auschwitz concentration camp. He has written that humor was an essential factor in his survival. Frankl, as a prisoner, encouraged his fellow prisoners to tell at least one funny story every day about something they intended to do after they were freed. Frankl wrote, "I never would have made it if I could not have laughed. It lifted me momentarily out of this horrible situation, just enough to make it livable."

After he was freed from Auschwitz, Frankl developed a school of psychotherapy called *logotherapy,* which incorporates humor as a major component of therapy. As a therapist, he encouraged patients to have fun with their problems instead of dealing with them through fighting or fleeing.

### Discover Life-Goal Benefits

Harvard professor Dr. George Vaillant studied two groups of aging men over time. Harvard graduates from the classes of 1939 through 1943 made up the first group. A large number of men from inner-city Boston comprised the second group. The men began their participation in the study when they were in their teens. They are now in their eighties. Vaillant concluded that the best predictors of successful aging are income, physical health, and *joy in living*. He discovered that "mature defenses" are what enable a person to achieve a good income, joy in living, and good health; these defenses include the ability to postpone gratification, future-mindedness, altruism, and humor.[20]

I heartily recommend that you find things you enjoy doing, and then do them frequently! Read an interesting novel, get absorbed in a stimulating conversation, spend time with an old friend, work on a hobby. Take time each day to do something that you truly enjoy doing.

Usually those activities or causes are ones that you pursue with a passion. Your passionate pursuit might be playing the piano, gardening, or spending time with your grandchildren. It might be volunteer work that you do at a hospital or day-care center or in building houses for the homeless. Your passionate pursuit might be taking short-term mission trips, knitting blankets for newborn babies, or rescuing lost pets. Whatever your passion, find ways of practicing it frequently.

### Have a Purpose, and Pursue It

Gratification comes from the pursuit of something that you believe has meaning and value. What's your reason for getting up in the morning? What keeps you interested in life? What gives you a feeling of fulfillment—a sense that you have done something good for others? Find an outlet for your natural gifts and talents, and then give yourself away to others.

---

FIND AN OUTLET FOR YOUR NATURAL GIFTS AND
TALENTS, AND THEN GIVE YOURSELF AWAY TO OTHERS.

---

### Cut Out the Criticism, Sarcasm, and Negative Jokes

Your parents probably taught you that if people aren't laughing when you are laughing, they very likely perceive that you are laughing *at* them rather than *with* them. Such laughter is hurtful, not healthful.

Just as there are differences in smiles, so there are differences in humor. Some humor is healthful, some isn't. There is humor that does not produce healing laughter. When one aims to increase, through humor, differences that are cultural, religious, sexual, racial, or political, such humor is nearly always hurtful, not healthful.

The cruel humorist makes a living out of sarcasm, ridicule, and degrading others. Such a humorist seeks to offend, and it is easy to see how others truly take offense at his words. The cruel humorist can leave a person feeling defeated, deflated, knocked down, or otherwise hurt. Humor that is cruel, cutting, condescending, or hurtful does not produce healthy emotions or positive effects in the physical body.

Positive humor unites hearts. The end result is laughter that leaves out no one and results in optimism and an upbeat attitude.

## If You Are Married, Stay Married

The National Opinion Research Center surveyed thirty-five thousand Americans over a thirty-year period and found that 40 percent of married individuals said they were "very happy." Only 24 percent of unmarried, divorced, separated, or widowed people said they were "happy" or "very happy."[21]

Marriage, more than jobs or finances, is associated with happiness. Marriage is actually one of the strongest predictors of happiness. Married individuals have the least amount of depression, followed by those who have never married, followed by those divorced only once, followed by people living with one another apart from marriage vows, followed by people who have been divorced twice or more than twice.[22]

Why do I share this information with you? Because as the national divorce rate has increased and marriage has declined in our society, the amount of depression has increased. It certainly would be foolish to suggest that all marriages produce happiness. They don't. On the other hand, those who are in happy, good marriages usually state that there's nothing better in life.

## AND NOW . . .

Let me ask you these final questions: How pleasant can you make today? For yourself? For those you love? For total strangers around you? I truly believe that the more you give away joy—including smiles and words of encouragement—the more you will feel joy welling up within. Try it!

# 15

## PEACE CAN FLOW LIKE A RIVER OF HEALTH

Jack came into my office in a rush and sat down so quickly and with such a thud that I thought he might break the chair. His first words were, "How long do you think this appointment is going to take?" I replied, "If time is the issue, then time is probably *the* issue."

He didn't seem to hear me. "You have no idea what kind of day I've been having." Without prompting, he proceeded to tell me everything he had done that day. He probably listed more than fifty things, from circling the parking lot three times before he found a space, to hitting absolutely every red light on the way in to work, to closing a major deal after four phone calls to three continents. And it was only three o'clock in the afternoon! He also went on to tell me all he still had to do before he could fall into bed—and it seemed to me as if he still had forty things on the list. I was exhausted just listening to him.

Jack was definitely a type A personality, he definitely had "hurry sickness," and he definitely was stuck in a permanent overdrive stress response. I rarely have encountered anybody quite so uptight and tense.

### OUR NEED TO RELAX

Overall, we have a great need as a nation to relax more. Very few people who are ill give themselves either time or space to heal fully.

Decades ago, before we had the cure for a number of diseases, people who became extremely ill with tuberculosis and other serious conditions went to sanatoriums. A sanatorium was a medical facility where a person mainly tried to recover strength and health. Some people today may think of these facilities as medical resorts or even medical spas, although they did not have the recreational facilities we tend to associate with a resort. The philosophy of medical personnel at a sanatorium was that people needed to relax before their immune systems could become strong, and a healthy immune system was necessary for the body to recharge and rejuvenate itself. This, in turn, the doctors regarded as the only means by which a person could overcome many types of diseases.

In today's world, with medical costs on the rise and medical insurance and HMO plans allowing for less and less hospital time, many people leave hospitals "quicker and sicker" than ever before. Often, people resume hectic lifestyles before their bodies have recovered fully from surgeries, pregnancies, or major infections.

In contrast, I know one woman whose company had a lenient return-to-work policy and she actually scheduled a surgery she may not have needed in order to have the two-month break her company allowed. She said, "I'm looking forward to this time off work so I can relax and do things with my daughter that I haven't been able to do for years."

Tension is a major factor in our lives. And it's a major factor underlying not only recovery times from illnesses, but also the onset of illnesses.

## SYMPATHETIC OR PARASYMPATHETIC?

Every muscle and every organ in the body has a sympathetic or stress state. It also has a parasympathetic or relaxed state. In the stress state, muscle fibers contract or tighten, and blood vessels constrict, driving up blood pressure.

In the relaxed state, muscle fibers lengthen, allowing the small blood vessels in the muscles to open up, which improves the flow of blood and much-needed oxygen to the muscles. This, in turn, helps deliver energy to the muscles and remove toxins from the muscles. In a relaxed state, lymphatic fluid flow rises, which increases the removal of cellular waste products and allows soft tissues to heal.

Many people who are chronically stressed have such constriction of their blood vessels that their hands and feet become cold. Others may develop reflex sympathetic dystrophy (RSD), a disabling condition characterized by severe pain, swelling, and tight, shiny skin. Excessive sympathetic discharge is its cause, which leads to constriction of the blood vessels and a decrease in the blood and oxygen flow to the extremities. RSD usually follows a surgical procedure, but it also can be a chronic stress response.

Both the parasympathetic nervous system and the sympathetic nervous system are parts of the autonomic nervous system. The parasympathetic system is active when an individual is in a relaxed, nonthreatened state. It conserves energy, which allows for strengthening, rejuvenating, regenerating processes in the entire body, including the immune system, cardiovascular system, GI tract, musculoskeletal system, nervous system, and almost every other system in the body.

Let me briefly summarize what each of these systems stimulates:

| Parasympathetic Stimulation | Sympathetic Stimulation |
| --- | --- |
| Decrease in heart rate | Increase in heart rate |
| Decreased force of contraction of the heart | Increased force of contraction of the heart |
| Decrease in blood pressure | Increase in blood pressure |
| Bronchoconstriction | Bronchodilation |
| Increase in digestive function | Decrease in digestive function |

| | |
|---|---|
| Increase in secretions in digestive tract | Decrease in secretions in digestive tract |
| Vasodilation (dilations or relaxing of blood vessels | Vasoconstriction (constriction of blood vessels) |
| Does not affect sweat glands | Increases sweating |
| Causes pupillary constriction | Causes pupillary dilation |

The Institute of HeartMath is an organization that researches the effects of positive emotions on physiology, quality of life, and performance. It helps individuals reduce stress and rejuvenate health. It provides prevention and intervention strategies for improving emotional health, decisionmaking, learning skills, and violence reduction in communities, families, and schools.

Researchers at this institute have shown that negative emotions lead to an increased disorder of the autonomic nervous system, which leads to erratic and less "coherent" heart rhythms. Positive emotions such as appreciation, love, care for others, and harmony result in more coherent heart rhythms.[1] For more information about HeartMath, visit their Web site at www.heartmath.com.

The rhythm of the heart is actually a balance of the parasympathetic and sympathetic nervous systems. An irregular beat, therefore, reflects an imbalance in these two systems. The goal of relaxation is to restore this balance, usually by decreasing those elements that trigger the sympathetic nervous system (which accelerates the heart rate) and enhancing the performance of the parasympathetic nervous system. (which slows down the heart rate)

Many people think of relaxation in terms of *unwinding*. Perhaps a better image would be to think of relaxation in terms of *balancing*.

I strongly urge you to clean your plate of things that you do not have to do. I sometimes ask my patients to consider this question: "What would you choose to do, and not do, if you had only six months to live?" Most people quickly come up with a list of things they *have* to do, would like to do, and then a few things they definitely would no longer do. I encourage them to take a look at those things they would no longer do and to drop them from their lives *immediately*. Then, I recommend that they use that freed-up time and energy to do a few things they would *like* to do.

So what would you do if you suddenly realized you had only six months to live?

SO WHAT WOULD YOU DO IF YOU SUDDENLY REALIZED
YOU HAD ONLY SIX MONTHS TO LIVE?

There's a balance of work and rest (including play and recreation) that's right for you. Choose to line up your commitments to achieve that balance.

## RELAXATION AS A FORM OF HEALTH TREATMENT

Relaxation has been a treatment for thousands of years. Hippocrates advocated massage in the fourth century B.C. to help people relax. Chinese medical texts written more than four thousand years ago contain information about massage as a health practice.

Edmund Jacobson introduced a technique now called "progressive relaxation" in the 1930s as a treatment for nervous disorders, fatigue, and generalized weakness.[2] This was one of the earliest relaxation techniques in Western medicine.

Over twenty-five years ago, Dr. Herbert Benson, a Harvard cardiologist, described a physiological reaction that he called the "relaxation response." This response was believed to be the opposite of the fight-or-flight response. The techniques he suggested include breathing exercises, progressive muscle relaxation, visualization and imagery, meditation, massage, aerobic exercise, music therapy, aromatherapy, humor therapy, stretching exercises, prayer, and a number of other techniques to stimulate the parasympathetic nervous system.[3]

In 1960, John Lilly found that he could induce a relaxation response if he allowed the person to rest in a "float chamber." This therapy involved spending an hour or so lying in a dark, quiet float tank suspended in a warm solution of water and Epsom salts about ten inches deep and so dense that the body seemed to float effortlessly. These tanks have a temperature of around ninety-three degrees Fahrenheit. The warm fluid environment frees the heart, nervous system, brain, and muscles from 90 percent of their workload and this, in turn, stimulates the parasympathetic nervous system. Lilly has found that heart rates and blood pressure normalize; muscle tension, back pain, and other pain associated with muscle groups decrease; efficiency of the cardiovascular system improves; oxygen and blood flow to all tissues increases; the immune system grows stronger; and recovery accelerates in people who have been injured or who have overexercised.[4]

The good news is that you don't need a therapist or a float tank in order to learn how to relax. You can learn simple methods and practices to generate a relaxation response. The basics you need are a quiet environment, a positive attitude, and comfortable clothing.

Several techniques work well for just about any person.

*Deep Breathing*

Those who are nervous or have been in an accident generally display rapid, shallow breathing. People who are agitated or are under severe stress tend to hold their breath. I experienced this just recently in a visit to my dentist. As he began to anesthetize around the tooth he intended to work on, I suddenly became aware that I was holding my breath and was very tense.

A person who continues to hold his breath and alternate this with rapid, shallow breathing may shift into hyperventilation, which is uncontrollable shallow, rapid breathing.

We should be aware of how we breathe at all times. Two types of breathing are possible—chest breathing and abdominal breathing. The better of these two is abdominal breathing.

Abdominal breathing produces improved oxygenation of the blood, which allows more oxygen to get to the muscles. This helps muscles relax. It also has a calming effect on the brain and nervous system; it relieves pain and stress.

To learn abdominal breathing I recommend that you lie down on your back in a comfortable position with your knees bent. (Once you have learned abdominal breathing, you can perform it standing, sitting, lying down, or moving about.)

Next, place your left hand on your abdomen and your right hand on your chest. Notice how your hands move as you breathe in and out.

Now try chest breathing so you see the contrast. In chest breathing, it is the shoulders that tend to go up and down with each breath, as opposed to the abdominal cavity moving in and out.

To get into the proper rhythm of abdominal breathing, first practice filling your lower lungs. Breathe with an effort at pushing out your left hand and causing your stomach and abdominal cavity area to expand. Your right hand on your chest should remain still. Some people like to put a telephone book on their abdomen while they are learning this type of breathing. As you inhale, the phone book should rise.

Inhale until you feel your stomach and abdominal cavity expanding to the point of also expanding your chest and rib cage.

Continue breathing this way for a couple of minutes. Make sure your breathing is slow and steady. Your breathing should be like the rolling waves of the sea, rising and falling in rhythm.

If you have not learned to breathe in this way, you may become dizzy if you try to get up too quickly. Rise slowly.

Usually a few minutes of abdominal breathing will leave a person feeling relaxed and calm—this amounts to about ten slow, deep, smooth breaths. I instruct my patients to inhale through their noses and exhale through their mouths.

A friend who once had a problem with alcohol taught me a variation on this breathing technique. He claimed this type of breathing had enabled him to stop drinking. Basically, he chose to breathe rather than drink.

Again, this exercise begins by lying down in a comfortable position with knees bent. Press your finger on one nostril to compress it and inhale a deep breath through the opposite nostril. Start the breath in the abdominal area and then move it upward to the chest and shoulders. Hold the breath for five seconds. Then compress the opposite nostril and exhale the air through the opposite nostril. When all the air has been exhaled, release the compression and repeat the process, switching nostrils. Continue this process for two to five minutes. This technique can decrease stress and tension significantly. Practicing abdominal breathing also is very effective as a "time out" measure to avoid saying something when you are angry that you will later regret.

### Progressive Muscle Relaxation

Therapists have used biofeedback for decades to help people to relax and to help control chronic pain, relieve migraine and tension headaches, and lessen tension and stress. Biofeedback therapists usually measure skin temperature, heart rate, blood pressure, electrical impulses to muscles, and so forth.

However, progressive muscle relaxation is a simple technique that any person can learn. Since most people have become so accustomed to muscles being tense that they no longer can identify them, you start the technique by tightening a particular muscle group . . . and then relaxing that particular muscle group. In other words, clench your fist for five seconds. Then release your fist, relaxing it as much as possible. Then, clench your shoulder muscles for five seconds, and relax your shoulder muscles, releasing all tension as much as possible until your muscles feel limp.

Begin doing this by lying or sitting quietly in a comfortable position. Close your eyes. Tighten and relax each muscle group you can identify, beginning at your feet and progressing upward to your face. As you tighten and release muscles, focus on your breathing, and practice abdominal breathing. Breathe slowly as you perform this relaxation exercise.

After you have gone from the muscles in your toes to the muscles of your forehead, give yourself a total body check to see if there is any area of your body that still seems to be tight. Redo the clenching and relaxing process in that area. Are your calves, thighs, hips and buttocks, abdomen, back, hands, biceps, shoulders, neck, and face all relaxed?

We generally experience relaxation as a feeling of limpness and heaviness. When the total body is relaxed, you'll probably feel like a "limp lump"—the phrase used by one woman who learned this technique and practiced it often.

This total exercise from toe to forehead should take about ten to twenty minutes. When you finish, sit quietly for a few minutes, first with your eyes closed and then with your eyes open. Do not stand for a few minutes.

Before you stand up, complete the exercise by raising your hands overhead and stretching them as far as they will go. Simultaneously push your feet out and down as far as they will go. Stretch and slowly count to ten. Repeat this if necessary.

Don't worry if you aren't completely successful the first time you try this. Distracting thoughts can occur, but try to ignore them and return to your focus on your own breathing.

If you are under a lot of stress, you may want to practice this technique once or twice a day, but not within two hours after a meal since the digestive process can interfere with the generation of a relaxation response.

Various audiotapes are available to help a person move through the different muscle groups. You may want to get one of those tapes.

## Yoga

A number of different kinds of yoga courses are available. Yoga exercises promote flexibility and strength in the body. They also teach a form of controlled breathing that helps release muscle tension. I do *not* recommend practicing yoga as a Hindu-related religious practice, which involves various forms of chanting and meditation. I recommend it only as a method of stretching and relaxing.

## Visualization and Imagery

We all practice mental imagery and visualization on a daily basis even if we aren't aware that we are doing so. Daydreaming and imagining are visualization techniques.

One of the visualization exercises I recommend to people is this: Imagine yourself sitting in a very warm Jacuzzi bath. Steam is rising off the water, but the water is not too hot to be comfortable. See yourself as slowly sinking into the whirlpool water. Feel the blood vessels of your hands dilating as blood flows to your hands and feet, warming them.

See yourself sitting in this water, enjoying the feel of the pulsating bubbles all around you. As much as possible, visualize color and beautiful foliage all around you.

Another visualization exercise invites you to see yourself lying in a warm meadow with a gentle breeze flowing over you. See yourself surrounded by hundreds of small, fragrant flowers. Nearby is a gently flowing brook. Hear the sound of the water and the birds singing in the trees nearby. See the white clouds slowly moving overhead against the backdrop of a brilliant blue sky. Inhale the scent of honeysuckle in the air.

Or visualize yourself walking along a beach, with warm wet sand under your feet and gently lapping waves to your side. Or see yourself sitting on the back porch of a log cabin at night next to a moonlit lake, listening to the crickets chirping and the bullfrogs croaking.

As a part of visualization techniques, you should focus on your breathing. It is also possible to engage in tense-and-relax muscle relaxation while lying in your imaginary meadow.

A ten-minute visualization break is like a minivacation: it allows your mind and heart to get away from the stress of the day.

A TEN-MINUTE VISUALIZATION BREAK IS LIKE A MINIVACATION: IT ALLOWS YOUR MIND AND HEART TO GET AWAY FROM THE STRESS OF THE DAY.

## Meditation

Meditation is of two general types. One type is guided meditation, which involves another person asking you to "see" various images on a relaxed journey of some type, perhaps through a forest or across a small footbridge. This is one of my patients' favorite relaxation techniques.

The other type of meditation aims at emptying the mind of stressful thoughts by focusing on one word, phrase, or a repetitive song. Meditation compels a person to become absorbed in the present moment. Many people are absorbed with thoughts of their pasts, including the hurried and stressful events of their immediate presents, or in thoughts and plans for their futures. Children are usually totally caught up in the present moment and as a result, they have very little stress, more laughter and fun, and far fewer chronic or stress-related diseases.

Three different focuses of meditation are common:

1. *Concentrated meditation,* which requires a person to focus on the sound of his breathing while repeating a meaningful word or phrase or concentrating on a particular mental image.

2. *Awareness meditation,* which requires a person to focus on a particular feeling or bodily sensation.

3. *Expressive meditation,* which requires a person to concentrate on a rhythmic physical activity, such as jogging or dancing. A person who is jogging can actually reach a meditative state of calm by concentrating on the up-and-down cadence of his feet striking the pavement.

My favorite forms of meditation are imagery meditation, meditating on Scripture, and Freeze-Frame, by HeartMath. Freeze-Frame differs from other forms of meditation because you learn to shift your focus from your head to your heart. While focusing on your heart, you re-experience a feeling of appreciation, joy, compassion, or love. From more information on Freeze-Frame, refer to www.heartmath.com.

Meditation has helped people manage chronic pain, relieve insomnia and nausea, and treat substance-abuse disorders. Some studies have shown promise for meditation as a technique for lowering blood pressure and possibly preventing heart attacks.[5]

### Prayer

Research has shown prayer to be very useful in inducing the relaxation response. Many individuals seek comfort in prayer during stressful times. Some people use repetitive prayers, such as phrases from the Scriptures that they repeat slowly or the Lord's prayer. One of the most popular of these is the simple prayer, "Lord Jesus Christ, have mercy upon me." Others find the greatest calm in a complete venting to God of all one is feeling deep inside, followed by a time of giving thanks and praise to God.

Some people I know couple praying with reading aloud God's promises from the Bible. Still others couple praying with seeing Jesus as taking a heavy load off their shoulders and strapping it to His own back. These people visualize 1 Peter 5:6–7, which says, "Humble yourselves under the mighty hand of God . . . casting all your care upon Him, for He cares for you."

You can also combine soothing music with meditation, visualization, or prayer. Research has shown that one's religious faith and practices, including prayer, reading Scriptures, and attending worship services, may decrease the impact of emotional stress in daily life and lessen the more serious stress of illness.[6]

### Massage

One of the oldest health practices is massage. I commonly recommend that my patients have one or two massages a week, especially if they are excessively stressed or have chronic pain, fibromyalgia, or any other disease heavily influenced by stress.

The skin has thousands of receptors that send messages through the nervous system to the brain to induce a feeling of relaxation, comfort, and well-being. Massage can trigger the release of endorphins, which are the body's natural pain relievers. Regular massage can also lower amounts of cortisol and epinephrine, the stress hormones. Massage certainly is helpful in releasing muscle tension, which can help with circulation.

In the late 1950s Tom Bowen, an Australian industrial engineer, developed a particular soft-tissue therapy. Bowen worked with junior football clubs in Victoria, Australia, as a masseure, and he discovered that he had extreme hypersensitivity in his fingers and hands that enabled him to find the blockages in the neuromuscular system. By 1975, he was treating approximately thirteen thousand people a year with incredible success. The Bowen technique seems to work primarily by balancing the two aspects of the autonomic nervous system.[7] You may want to seek out a masseuse or masseur who has been trained in the Bowen technique. For more information on Bowen Therapy, consult the Web site at www.bowen.org.

### Aerobic Exercise

Brisk walking, cycling, swimming, rowing, dancing, jogging, and other aerobic exercises actually help relax the body, provided you do not exercise at too high an intensity.

### A Daily Relaxation Time

Other lesser known and less-researched techniques to help induce relaxation include aromatherapy and humor therapy. I have found in my practice that the specific technique a patient uses isn't as important as the fact that he practices relaxation *daily*. Choose the technique that works best for you, and use it regularly.

### Sleep: The Ultimate Relaxation Time

It is also critically important that you sleep seven to nine hours a night. Aim for eight to nine hours of sleep on weekend nights. Too many Americans today are living their lives in a sleep-deprived state. Physical stress, and ultimately stress-related diseases, are the consequences.

More than half of all Americans suffer from insomnia at least a few times a week.[8] Excessive stress, anxiety, and depression are commonly at the root of insomnia. Here are some simple suggestions for improving your sleep:

*Limit your bedroom to sleep.* Don't study, eat, work on the computer, watch television, or do any other "work" activity in your bedroom. By limiting this room to sleep only, you send a signal to your body that entering this room begins the go-to-sleep process of unwinding and relaxing.

*Go to bed and get up at approximately the same time each day.* Do this even on weekends. This regular routine conditions your internal clock.

*Keep your bedroom uncluttered.* This will help you avoid distractions that may cause stress.

*Keep your bedroom dark.* Make sure that no light shines in from the street or even from a nightlight. You may need to cover up a bright digital clock. Start dimming the lights in other rooms of your house in early evening.

*Shut off the noisemakers.* Unplug the phone in your bedroom. Use earplugs if necessary to keep honking horns or sirens from interrupting your sleep. (On stormy nights, however, you may want to leave out the earplugs so you can hear a storm-warning siren.)

*Do not drink beverages with caffeine (coffee, tea, soft drinks).* Also don't eat chocolate, spicy foods, or fatty foods before bedtime. And avoid medications containing caffeine or stimulants in the evening.

*Keep your bedroom at a comfortable temperature.* For most people this is around seventy degrees Fahrenheit.

*Don't exercise just before bedtime.* Do your exercise in the late afternoon or early evening, but not within two hours of bedtime.

*Select a comfortable pillow and mattress.* Use a mattress that allows you to sleep soundly with good body support for your spine.

*Practice a relaxation technique prior to bedtime.*

If you do awaken in the night, get up only if you absolutely must. If you have trouble falling back to sleep, try a relaxation technique as you lie in bed. You may want to memorize and then recite these verses if you awaken in the night:

- I will both lie down in peace, and sleep;
  For You alone, O LORD, make me dwell in safety. (Ps. 4:8)

- It is vain for you to rise up early,
  To sit up late,

To eat the bread of sorrows;
For so He gives His beloved sleep. (Ps. 127:2)

- When you lie down, you will not be afraid;
Yes, you will lie down and your sleep will be sweet. (Prov. 3:24)

*Keep the Sabbath day.* A time of prolonged rest during daylight hours is also part of God's plan for the human body.

Many people seem to think they are honoring the Sabbath by not going into the office or factory, but in reality, they work on that day by running to the mall to shop or doing house- or yardwork. We Americans tend to be 24/7 people: on the go twenty-four hours a day, seven days a week.

God intended that the Sabbath day be a time of quiet and peaceful meditation and conversation about God's Word—a time with family and close friends, void of hurry, work, or any activities that required prolonged exertion mentally or physically. The command to "remember the Sabbath day and keep it holy" appears more times in the Bible than any of the other Ten Commandments.

Even if you aren't feeling particularly stressed right now, begin to practice relaxation response techniques regularly to *avoid* getting stressed. A basketball team doesn't start to practice free throws the day of the postseason tournament game. The team has practiced free throws daily for months so that if one player finds himself on the foul line at the end of the game, with the score tied, he is ready! One person has estimated that a good college basketball player shoots at least ten thousand practice free throws during his college career.

We need to prepare ourselves for stress in the same way: we need to be able to move quickly into a relaxation response technique of deep breathing, progressive muscle relaxation, visualization, meditation, prayer, and so forth. Then when a stressful situation hits us, we know how to respond quickly and effectively to counteract a stress buildup.

## BETTER FOR THE WHOLE OF YOU

Experiencing relaxation is a part of experiencing deep inner peace. It isn't the whole story; peace also comes from forgiveness, the flow of love in your life, and truthful thinking. Relaxation, however, very often puts you in a greater frame of mind and heart to extend forgiveness, feel the flow of love, and confront difficult emotions.

Relaxation helps a person perform better, work better, give more, accomplish more, and be open to laughing more.

It may sound like an odd juxtaposition of words, but relaxation is worth the effort. If you learn to relax, you will be in a position to experience much greater health.

# | 16 |

# RESTORING VITALITY:
# THE LOVE CONNECTION

In my medical practice, I routinely take time to sit down with patients and interview them to discover the emotional events that may have preceded their illnesses. One patient was named Charlie. He was a fifty-seven-year-old machinist who had battled lymphoma for years. Lymphoma is a form of cancer of the lymph nodes and lymphatic fluid. Charlie was absolutely thrilled when his treatments were complete and he received a clean bill of health. He felt as if he had been given a second chance at life, and he told me he planned to "make it count."

Tragically, Charlie went home from work at his shop several weeks later to discover an empty house. About half of the furniture had been moved out that morning while he was working a double shift. The kitchen was completely bare, except for a note attached to divorce papers that had been left on a counter near the sink.

Charlie's wife, the much younger and very attractive Carla, had left him for another man. She wrote in her note that she couldn't handle "the burden of his sickness." Brokenhearted, Charlie was overcome by emotions he could not seem to vent. Less than three months after this experience, his cancer came out of remission with a raging fury, and he died within a year.

Charlie's experience was one more vivid example to me of the link between emotion and disease.

When my wife, Mary, and I attended his funeral, I felt great sadness. Charlie, in my opinion, did not die of lymphoma. He died of a broken heart. Would Charlie have lived if he had been able to prevail over the toxic emotions he felt in the wake of Carla's leaving? We'll never know.

Would Charlie's cancer have stayed in remission if his wife had stayed by his side? I genuinely believe that might have been a strong possibility. After seeing situations such as Charlie's again and again, I am thoroughly convinced that the body absorbs stormy emotions and if they remain there, they set in motion a series of biochemical reactions that eventually end in disease.

Mother Teresa said that the greatest disease of mankind is the absence of love. I couldn't agree more.

Jesus thought so much of love that He spent a significant part of His last night before His crucifixion talking to His disciples about it. He said: "A new commandment I give to you, that you love one another; as I have loved you, that you also love one another. By this all will know that you are My disciples, if you have love for one another" (John 13:34–35).

> JESUS THOUGHT SO MUCH OF LOVE THAT HE SPENT A SIGNIFICANT PART OF HIS LAST NIGHT BEFORE HIS CRUCIFIXION TALKING TO HIS DISCIPLES ABOUT IT.

## LOVING YOURSELF

The Bible issues strong admonition that we are to love others as we love ourselves (see Matt. 22:39; Lev. 19:18). I believe an ability to love begins in receiving God's love—usually in the form of His mercy and forgiveness—and then learning to love ourselves.

How does a person love himself? In many ways, this relates to self-esteem—to having feelings of worthiness, value, and purpose in life. In the physical realm, the way we generally show love to our bodies is to pamper them. The entire spa industry has been built on just that premise. Most people I know intuitively agree that it's important for us to care for our bodies, which includes eating the right foods, getting sufficient rest, and treating ourselves occasionally to a massage, a facial, or a body scrub.

I don't know anybody who doesn't enjoy a good back rub, foot rub, or neck rub, especially after a high-stress day. We human beings enjoy the sensation of being touched in a gentle, loving, and stimulating way. We enjoy human contact, but we also enjoy the feelings we have through the nerve endings of our skin.

In like manner, we have a fondness for fabrics that are soft and comfortable against the skin. We like products that make our skin soft and pliable.

One of the foremost ways you can love yourself is to care for your skin. The way you treat your skin—and the way you allow others to touch you, literally as well as figuratively—is a great indicator of health.

Now, I'm not advocating a heavy emphasis on cosmetics; rather, I'm advocating the *health* of the skin as a reflection of the *healthy* way in which we respond to the sensation of touch.

In turn, the person who has a genuine concern for the health of his skin usually has a concern for the health of his entire being.

The person who loves himself enjoys being touched by others in pure, godly ways.

Ask yourself:

- "Am I truly open to being touched by others?"

- "Am I willing to express my own emotions in physical, touching ways?"

## BEWARE OF THE ADDICTIVE NATURE OF ROMANTIC LOVE

Many people in our society place a high emphasis on romantic love. They seek out and ardently desire love that shows itself in candlelight, flowers, soft words, and ultimately, a sexual encounter.

The kind of love that truly heals us emotionally and physically is not romantic love, but rather the unconditional love that comes from God. The love that heals is not sexual in nature, but spiritual.

It is interesting to me that research is showing that romantic love can act much like an addictive agent. Helen Fisher, a research professor of anthropology at Rutgers University, is among many scientists who believe that first meeting "someone special" triggers a flush of stimulants to the brain. These hormones, especially dopamine and norepinephrine, impact the same brain centers as cocaine and produce similarly euphoric feelings. These brain chemicals can cause lovers to lose their appetites and their desire for sleep if they simply think about their significant others.[1]

Nora Volkow, associate director for life sciences at Brookhaven National Laboratory in New York, has analyzed the behaviors of drug addicts and people in love and has found striking parallels. She has said, "When a person is passionately in love it is extremely exciting and provocative, and if the loved one is not there, distressing." She believes that taking a drug or being in love raises an addict's dopamine levels to the "perfect zone." Volkow has also stated that recent research studies reveal that when a drug addict is high and when someone is in love and looks at a photo of his beloved, he activates the same regions of the brain, including the frontal cortex.[2]

Researchers at the University College in London, Andreas Bartles and Semir Zeki, recently recorded changes in the brains of people who described themselves as "truly and madly" in love. These researchers used a functional magnetic resonance imager to scan the brains of these seventeen lovebirds. They also used lie detectors to screen out those who might be exaggerating their feelings. When the team showed volunteers photos of their lovers, the results were dramatic. Four small areas of the brain lit up instantly— the same areas that have been shown to respond to euphoria-inducing drugs.[3]

Phenylethylamine (PEA) is one of the main stimulants of the nervous system and is actively released when a person claims to be "truly and madly" in love. PEA triggers endorphins, the body's natural analgesic. It also supercharges the actions of dopamine, the brain's primary neurotransmitter involved in sexual arousal. Researchers believe that PEA is responsible for the restless, giddy sensation people popularly refer to as being "lovesick."[4]

The bad news here is that people who think this initial rush associated with love is true love tend to go from one brain-chemical high to the next. They become addicted to the feelings of love rather than move into a more mature relationship, i.e., shared values and a commitment to shared goals and a shared life. For a truly loving relationship to last, lovers must moderate mad passion with understanding, mutual respect, genuine empathy, companionship, and other healthy aspects of a relationship that seek to *give* to the other person as much or more than to *get* from the other person.

Joanne Tangedahl addressed this in her book *A New Blueprint for Marriage*. She noted that if a "love addiction" doesn't pass, it becomes progressively worse. She wrote: "You stop having a sense of well-being and that wonderful feeling of oneness. You begin to feel desperate, with a need to be with, to see, to possess the other person. This need is so powerful, strong, and compelling people often call this love. It is not love, it is addiction."[5]

Very often when love addicts fall out of love, they feel a strong need to replace their addiction with another stimulant until they can find another person to whom they feel strongly attracted. Unfortunately, these other substitutes can promote an even stronger physical addiction, one that may be very difficult to break or one that causes more damage to the person physically, emotionally, mentally, or spiritually.

I have found it interesting that chocolate shares some of the same properties as addictive love. I've mentioned that scientists have isolated PEA, a stimulant of the nervous system. PEA also appears in chocolate and is released in the brain during times of emotional euphoria. When a person is in passionate "love"—or when one consumes a significant amount of chocolate—levels of

PEA increase. Perhaps it isn't such a mystery after all why giving chocolate candy has been linked with courtship through the years.[6]

## EXPERIENCING GENUINE, HEALING LOVE

At times people have asked me, "How can I tell if I am experiencing genuine love in my life?" I point them to a passage in the New Testament. One of the most eloquent love descriptions of all time appears in the apostle Paul's first letter to the Corinthians:

> Love suffers long and is kind; love does not envy; love does not parade itself, is not puffed up; does not behave rudely, does not seek its own, is not provoked, thinks no evil; does not rejoice in iniquity, but rejoices in the truth; bears all things, believes all things, hopes all things, endures all things. Love never fails . . .
>
> And now abide faith, hope, love, these three; but the greatest of these is love. (1 Cor. 13:4–8, 13)

Let me briefly summarize and comment on the hallmark characteristics of love that Paul mentioned in this passage. To a great extent, love is evident in both the qualities it manifests and those it doesn't.

### Love Is Patient

Do you suffer from "hurry sickness" or impatience? A simple test of patience: how long does it take for you to honk your horn when you are sitting behind a driver who does not move after the light turns green? A truly patient person seldom honks, and if he does, it is usually with a gentle reminder tap. An impatient person is quick to lay on the horn.

### Love Is Kind

Our friend Carol Kornacki made an interesting comment regarding kindness. She pointed out that although Princess Diana was admittedly unfaithful to her husband, suffered from an eating disorder, and died while having an affair outside the bounds of marriage, no one defines her by those things. People remember her as being kind—as supporting charitable causes and visiting and touching people others perceived as untouchable. How quick are you to give a smile, your time, gifts, joy, and a listening ear to others?

### Love Is Not Jealous

It does not seek to control or manipulate others. Are you willing to allow others to share friendship with your friends? Are you quick to volunteer your possessions or your home for something that benefits others? Are you quick to applaud others who succeed or who are promoted or receive rewards?

### Love Is Not Proud or Boastful

Do you feel an overwhelming need to tell others about your achievements or possessions? Does the conversation always seem to come around to you—not because others ask but because you feel a need to tell?

### Love Is Not Rude

One of the great manifestations of love is courtesy. Unloving people rarely care about manners and they don't bother saying "please" or "thank you." How about you?

### Love Is Not Selfish

Being self-centered or selfish has very little to do with hoarding possessions or keeping them away from another person. Selfish people are those who insist on having their way. They expect others to give in to their demands. They are "my way or the highway" people. Are you quick to put the needs of others ahead of your needs?

### Love Does Not Keep Track of Wrongs

Loving people forgive quickly and easily and refuse to keep score against another person. Check your own heart. Are you holding something against another person? Do you feel you need to settle a score with someone?

### Love Is Quick to Believe the Best

Love doesn't gossip or look for flaws in other people. Love holds people in high regard and quickly overlooks a mistake. Do you find yourself jumping to the worst conclusions about people without giving them the benefit of the doubt?

### Love Desires Justice

Those who are loving want to see justice prevail for those who are victims. They find no pleasure in hearing about crime or violence. They have hearts that desire to help the innocent. Is there anybody about whom you find yourself saying, "He deserves what he got"?

### Love Never Fails

Love is constant. The truly loving person just keeps on loving, no matter what happens—no matter what others say or do, or the situation or circumstances. Love hangs in there. Have you given up on a person, convinced that he is destined for hard times or eternal punishment?

## MAKING THE CHOICE TO BE LOVING

After someone firebombed his home, Dr. Martin Luther King Jr. wrote, "The chain of reaction of evil—hate begetting hate, war producing more wars—must be broken, or we shall be plunged into the dark abyss of an annihilation . . . Love is the only force capable of transforming an enemy into a friend . . . By its very nature, hate destroys and tears down; by its very nature love creates and builds up."[7]

Walking in love is a choice. Acting on that choice takes effort. Love means *choosing* to turn yourself inside out for others, to turn your thinking upside down from the way the vast majority of people in the world think, and to go radically against what many people perceive to be basic human nature and pursue instead the nature of God. Making this choice to love sometimes means you have to suffer.

But here's the good news: suffering for the sake of love doesn't have to mean bearing emotional pain or stress-related disease. Emotional and stress-related physical suffering derive from hate. Those who love may endure hard times financially or socially; others may persecute them, even to the point of external blows on their bodies, but they do not suffer internally in the same ways as those who hate.

A person who makes a commitment to walk in love is a person who nearly always discovers he has made a decision of supreme quality.

> A PERSON WHO MAKES A COMMITMENT TO WALK IN LOVE
> IS A PERSON WHO NEARLY ALWAYS DISCOVERS HE HAS
> MADE A DECISION OF SUPREME QUALITY.

Walking in love requires not only an intentional, initial choice, but an ongoing intentional choice. Loving as God loves requires practice, practice, practice. So begin to practice patience and kindness. Practice not being jealous, proud, rude, or selfish.

## EXPRESSING HEALING LOVE TO OTHERS

It is not enough that you feel love in your heart. You must give away love. We do this in several basic ways:

- Words of affirmation to others. Be quick to give compliments or encouraging words in response to what another person does or says.

- The gift of time. There's an old saying that children spell love t-i-m-e. The same is true for spouses. Spending time with a person, without an agenda or task to accomplish, is love expressed.

- The giving of gifts. Find out what another person likes and then give that gift to him.

- Acts of service. Service is different from gift-giving. In gifts, the focus is on what brings pleasure to a person. Service focuses on what a person truly needs. What can you do to help the busiest person you love? The answer is likely an act of service: fixing dinner, mowing the lawn, picking up the laundry, or taking a package to the post office.

- Acts of physical affection. We are human beings who need touch. An act of love may be as simple as a kiss, hug, caress, pat on the back, or holding hands. It may be sexual intercourse with a spouse, or a long massage or back rub. We touch those we truly love—and always in a way that the other person perceives to be appropriate.

It isn't enough that we choose to express love in these ways. What's truly important is that we discover which expressions of love our loved ones most desire and most readily receive. Which form of love expression does the person you love seem to need or request most often?

One woman said to me, "I found great freedom in loving when I asked my husband, 'What is it that you really want from me?' His requests were very few—in fact, far fewer than I had thought they would be. I had been spending my time and energy and creativity doing all sorts of things that were totally meaningless to him. When I focused on doing what was meaningful . . . wow. He was quick to seek out ways of expressing his love that were meaningful to *me*!"

A friend of ours named Carol Kornacki recently received an invitation to speak at a very small church in her hometown. The church was one that she had never attended, but since the appeal came from a friend, she decided to go.

When Carol pulled up at the address given to her, she found that the building looked more like a shack than a church. She entered a musty chapel and took a seat on a tattered pew. As the congregation began to arrive, she couldn't help but notice how many of the people seemed to have some form of mental retardation.

A stocky preacher stood up to start the service. His shirt and tie looked as though he had spilled a good portion of his supper on them. The tail of his shirt hung out of his baggy pants in several places. His sermon was less than spectacular.

Carol spoke for a few moments and then the service was over. She noticed that people didn't leave. Instead, they formed something of a receiving line and waited patiently for the pastor to come their way. He stopped to give big bear hugs and words of encouragement to each person, sharing muffled laughter with a number of them. Carol said, "I saw the love of God in action. There was gentleness, kindness, goodness, and humility in this servant of the Master that brought tears to my eyes. This man had perfected the language of the heart."

The Bible includes Paul's desire for followers of Christ: "May the Lord make you increase and abound in love to one another and to all, just as we do to you, so that He may establish your hearts blameless in holiness before our God and Father at the coming of our Lord Jesus Christ with all His saints" (1 Thess. 3:12–13). That's my hope for you.

# Appendix A

## THE HOLMES-RAHE LIFE EVENT SCALE

This life-event scale can help you determine your overall stress level. You may be surprised to discover how much stress certain events create.

For each event that applies to you *at this time*, write the points in the space provided. If an event does *not* apply to you *at this time*, do not write anything in the blank.

You may have more total stress in your life than you think!

| | Points | Points in Your Life |
|---|---|---|
| Death of a spouse | 100 | _____ |
| Divorce | 73 | _____ |
| Marital separation | 65 | _____ |
| Jail term | 63 | _____ |
| Death of close family members | 63 | _____ |
| Personal injury or illness | 53 | _____ |
| Marriage | 50 | _____ |
| Fired at work | 47 | _____ |
| Marital reconciliation | 45 | _____ |
| Retirement | 45 | _____ |

| | | |
|---|---|---|
| Change in family member's health | 44 | _____ |
| Pregnancy | 40 | _____ |
| Sex difficulties | 39 | _____ |
| Addition to family | 39 | _____ |
| Business readjustment | 39 | _____ |
| Change in financial circumstances | 38 | _____ |
| Death of a close friend | 37 | _____ |
| Change to different line of work | 36 | _____ |
| Change in number of marital arguments | 35 | _____ |
| Mortgage or loan for major purchases | 31 | _____ |
| Foreclosure of mortgage or loan | 30 | _____ |
| Change in work responsibilities | 29 | _____ |
| Son or daughter leaving home | 29 | _____ |
| Trouble with in-laws | 29 | _____ |
| Outstanding personal achievement | 28 | _____ |
| Spouse begins or stops work | 26 | _____ |
| Starting or finishing school | 26 | _____ |
| Change in living conditions | 25 | _____ |
| Revision of personal habits | 24 | _____ |

| | | |
|---|---|---|
| Trouble with boss | 23 | _____ |
| Change in work hours or conditions | 20 | _____ |
| Change in residence | 20 | _____ |
| Change in schools | 20 | _____ |
| Change in recreational habits | 19 | _____ |
| Change in church activities | 19 | _____ |
| Change in social activities | 18 | _____ |
| Mortgage or loan for minor purchase (such as TV, car) | 17 | _____ |
| Change in sleeping habits | 16 | _____ |
| Change in number of family gatherings | 15 | _____ |
| Change in eating habits | 15 | _____ |
| Vacation | 13 | _____ |
| Christmas season | 12 | _____ |
| Minor violations of the law | 11 | _____ |
| Total Score: | | _____ |

*How Did You Score?*

Add your point values for all events that pertain to your current life.

300 or more: You stand an almost 80 percent chance of getting sick in the near future.

150–299: Your chances of becoming ill are about 50 percent.

149 or less:    Your chances of becoming ill are about 30 percent.

Your score may predict how you will act individually to a particular stressful circumstance. Those who have more total stress points, for example, tend to react in a more irritated, frustrated, angry, or depressed manner to any one stressful situation.

Reprinted from: Holmes, T. and Rahe, R.H., "Holmes-Rahe Social Readjustment Rating Scale," *Journal of Psychosomatic Research,* vol. 11:213–218, © 1967 with permission from Elsevier, Inc.

# Appendix B

## THE NOVACO ANGER INVENTORY

Read the list of twenty-five potentially upsetting situations described below. In the space provided, estimate the degree of annoyance or anger you believe you would experience in this situation, using this rating scale:

> 0 = Very little or no annoyance
>
> 1 = A little irritated
>
> 2 = Moderately upset
>
> 3 = Quite angry
>
> 4 = Very angry

1. You unpack an appliance you have just bought, plug it in, and discover that it doesn't work.  _____

2. A repairman who has you over a barrel overcharges you.  _____

3. Your boss singles you out for correction while ignoring the actions of others.  _____

4. Your car gets stuck in the snow.  _____

5. You talk to someone and he doesn't answer or acknowledge you.  _____

6. Someone pretends to be something he
   is not.                                        _____

7. While you are struggling to carry four        _____
   cups of coffee to your table at the
   cafeteria, someone bumps into you,
   spilling the coffee.

8. After you hang up your clothes,               _____
   someone knocks them to the floor and
   fails to pick them up.

9. A salesperson hounds you from the             _____
   moment you enter a store.

10. You have made arrangements to go             _____
    somewhere with a person who backs out
    at the last minute and leaves you hanging.

11. Someone jokes about or teases you.           _____

12. Your car stalls at a traffic light and the   _____
    driver behind you keeps blowing his horn.

13. You accidentally make a wrong turn in        _____
    a parking lot—as you get out of your car
    someone yells at you, "Where did you
    learn to drive?"

14. Someone makes a mistake and blames           _____
    you for it.

15. You are trying to concentrate but a          _____
    person near you continually taps his foot.

16. You lend someone an important book           _____
    or tool and he fails to return it.

17. You have had a busy day and the              _____
    person with whom you live starts to
    complain about how you forgot
    to do something you had agreed to do.

18. You are in a discussion with someone _____
    and a third person persists in interrupting
    to bring up a topic she knows very little
    about.

19. You are trying to discuss something _____
    important with your spouse, who doesn't
    give you a chance to express your feelings
    fully without interruption.

20. Someone sticks his nose into an _____
    argument you and another person are
    having.

21. You need to get somewhere quickly, but _____
    the car in front of you is going twenty-
    five miles per hour in a forty-mile-per-
    hour zone, and you can't pass.

22. You step on a wad of chewing gum. _____

23. A small group of people mocks you as _____
    you pass them.

24. In a hurry to get somewhere, you tear a _____
    garment on a sharp object.

25. You use all your change to make a _____
    phone call but are disconnected just
    after the party you are calling says,
    "Hello."

Total of all responses: _____

## How Did You Score?

0–45    The amount of anger and annoyance you generally
        experience is remarkably low. Very few people will
        have such a score. You are one of the calmest people
        in our society!

46–55   You are substantially more peaceful than the average person.

56–75   You respond to life's annoyances with an average amount of anger.

76–85   Your tendency is to react in an angry way to life's annoyances. You are more irritable than the average person.

86–100  You are a true champion of anger. Frequent, intense, furious reactions that do not quickly disappear probably plague you. You probably harbor negative feelings long after the initial insult has passed. You may have the reputation of being a "firecracker" or a "hothead." You may experience frequent tension headaches and elevated blood pressure. Your anger may get out of control at times, resulting in impulsive hostile outbursts. Your temper probably gets you into trouble. Only a few of the adult population react as intensely or angrily as you.

From: Novaco, R. W., *Anger Control: The Development and Evaluation of an Experimental Treatment* (Lexington, MA: DC Health, 1975). Used by permission.

# Appendix C

## THE ZUNG SELF-RATING DEPRESSION SCALE

### KEY TO SCORING THE ZUNG SELF-RATING DEPRESSION SCALE

Consult this key for the value (1-4) that correlates with patients' responses to each statement. Add up the numbers for a total score. Most people with depression score between 50 and 69. The highest possible score is 80.

| Make check mark (✓) in appropriate column. | A little of the time | Some of the time | Good part of the time | Most of the time |
|---|---|---|---|---|
| 1. I feel down-hearted and blue | 1 | 2 | 3 | 4 |
| 2. Morning is when I feel best | 1 | 2 | 3 | 4 |
| 3. I have crying spells or feel like it | 1 | 2 | 3 | 4 |
| 4. I have trouble sleeping at night | 1 | 2 | 3 | 4 |
| 5. I eat as much as I used to | 1 | 2 | 3 | 4 |
| 6. I still enjoy sex | 1 | 2 | 3 | 4 |
| 7. I notice that I am losing weight | 1 | 2 | 3 | 4 |
| 8. I have trouble with constipation | 1 | 2 | 3 | 4 |
| 9. My heart beats faster than usual | 1 | 2 | 3 | 4 |
| 10. I get tired for no reason | 1 | 2 | 3 | 4 |
| 11. My mind is as clear as it used to be | 1 | 2 | 3 | 4 |
| 12. I find it easy to do the things I used to | 1 | 2 | 3 | 4 |
| 13. I am restless and can't keep still | 1 | 2 | 3 | 4 |
| 14. I feel hopeful about the future | 1 | 2 | 3 | 4 |
| 15. I am more irritable than usual | 1 | 2 | 3 | 4 |
| 16. I find it easy to make decisions | 1 | 2 | 3 | 4 |
| 17. I feel that I am useful and needed | 1 | 2 | 3 | 4 |
| 18. My life is pretty full | 1 | 2 | 3 | 4 |
| 19. I feel that others would be better off off if I were dead | 1 | 2 | 3 | 4 |
| 20. I still enjoy the things I used to do | 1 | 2 | 3 | 4 |

## Scoring for the Zung Self-Rating Depression Scale

| Below 50 | Normal |
|---|---|
| 50-59 | Mild depression |
| 60-69 | Moderate to marked depression |
| 70 or higher | Severe depression |

# NOTES

Introduction

1. D. Wayne, "Reactions to Stress," found in *Identifying Stress,* a series offered by the Health-Net & Stress Management Web site, February 1998.

Chapter 1

1. P. Rosch, "Job Stress: America's Leading Adult Health Problem," *USA Today,* May 1991, 42–44.
2. Doc Childre and Howard Martin, *The HeartMath Solution* (San Francisco: HarperCollins, 1999), 55.
3. Quoted in H. Dreher, *The Immune Power Personality* (New York: Dutton, 1995), 15.
4. H. J. Eysenck, "Personality, Stress, and Anger: Prediction and Prophylaxis," *British Journal of Medical Psychology,* 61 (1988): 57–75.
5. M. A. Mittleman, M. Manclure, J. B. Sherwood, et al., "Triggering of Acute Myocardial Infarction Onset by Episodes of Anger," *Circulation,* 92 (1995): 1720–1725.
6. L. D. Kubzansky, I. Kawachi, A. Spirio III, et al., "Is Worrying Bad for Your Heart? A Prospective Study of Worry and Coronary Heart Disease in the Normative Aging Study," *Circulation,* 94 (1997): 818–824.
7. J. Dixon and J. Spinner, "Tensions Between Career and Interpersonal Commitments As a Risk Factor for Cardiovascular Disease Among Women," *Women and Health,* 17 (1991): 33–57.
8. B. W. Penninx, T. van Tilburg, D. M. Kriegsman, et al., "Effects of Social Support and Personal Coping Resources on Mortality in Older Age: The Longitudinal Aging Study Amsterdam," *American Journal of Epidemiology,* 146 (1997): 510–519.
9. T. G. Allison, D. E. Williams, T. D. Miller, et al., "Medical and Economic Costs of Psychologic Distress in Patients with Coronary Artery Disease," *Mayo Clinic Proceedings,* 70 (1995): 734–742.

Chapter 2

1. Candace Pert, et al., "Opiate Agonists and Antagonists Discriminated by Receptor Binding in the Brain," *Science,* 182 (1973): 1359–61.

2. Paul Pearsall, *The Pleasure Prescription* (Alameda, Calif.: Hunter House Publishers, 1996), 90.

3. B. Hafen, K. Frandsen, K. Karen, et al., *The Health Effects of Attitudes, Emotions, and Relationships* (Provo, Utah: EMS Associates, 1992).

4. W. Cannon, "The role of emotion in disease," *The Annals of Internal Medicine,* 9 (1936).

5. H. Selye, *The Stress of Life* (McGraw Hill, 1956).

6. A. Hart, *Adreneline and Stress* (Nashville: W Publishing Group, 1995).

7. C. Hiemke, "Circadian Variations in Antigen-Specific Proliferations of Human T Lymphocytes and Correlation to Cortisol Production," *Psychoneuroendocrinology,* 20 (1994): 335–342.

8. P. DeFeo, "Contribution of Cortisol to Glucose Counter-regulation in Humans," *American Journal of Physicology,* 257 (1989): E35–E42.

9. S. C. Manolagas, "Adrenal Steroids and the Development of Osteoporosis in the Oophorectomized Women," *Lancet,* 2 (1979): 597.

10. R. Beme, *Physiology,* 3$^{rd}$ ed. (St. Louis: Mosby, 1993).

11. P. Marin, "Cortisol Secretion in Relation to Body Fat Distribution in Obese Premenopausal Women," *Metabolism,* 41 (1992): 882–886.

12. D. S. Kerr, et al., "Chronic Stress-Induced Acceleration of Electrophysiologic and Morphometric Biomarkers of Hippocampal Aging," *Society of Neuroscience,* 11 (1991): 1316–1317; and R. Sapolsky, *Stress, the Aging Brain, and Mechanisms of Neuron Death* (Cambridge, Mass.: MIT Press, 1992).

13. Paul Pearsall, *The Pleasure Prescription,* 63.

14. Ibid.

15. Ibid.

CHAPTER 3

1. T. Holmes and R. Rahe, "The Social Readjustment Rating Scale," *Journal of Psychosomatic Research,* 11 (1967): 213–218.

2. Robert M. Sapolsky, *Why Zebras Don't Get Ulcers* (New York: W. H. Freeman, 1998), 49.

3. Al'abadie, et al., "The Relationship Between Stress and the Onset and Exacerbation of Psoriasis and Other Skin Conditions," *British Journal of Dermatology,* 199 (1994): 203.

4. J. Fulton, *Acne Rx* (James Fulton Publishing, 2001). Dr. Fulton is a renowned dermatologist who developed Retin A.

5. I. Grant, et al., "Severely Threatening Events and Marked Life Difficulties Preceding Onset or Exacerbation of Multiple Sclerosis," *Journal of Neurology, Neurosurgery and Psychiatry,* 52 (1989): 8–13.

6. A. J. Zautra, et al., "Examination of Changes in Interpersonal Stress as a Factor in Disease Exacerbation Among Women with Rheumatoid Arthritis," *Annals of Behavioral Medicine,* 19 (1997): 279–286.

7. Pearsall, *The Pleasure Prescription,* 66.

CHAPTER 4

1. M. Agnes, et al., eds., *Webster's New World College Dictionary,* 4$^{th}$ ed. (Foster City, Ca.: IDG Books Worldwide, 2001.)

2. Robert Elliott, *Is It Worth Dying For?* (New York: Bantam Books, 1989).
3. R. Williams et al., *Anger Kills* (NY: Harper Collins, 1993).
4. Ibid.
5. W.F. Enos, et al., "Coronary disease among U.S. soldiers killed in action in Korea," *JAMA,* 152 (1953): 1090–93.
6. Eversol, et al., "Hostility and increased risk of mortality and acute myocardial infarction: the mediating role of behavioral risk factors," *AM J Epidemial,* 146 (2) (1997): 142–152.
7. A. Spiro, *Health Psychology,* Nov. 22. webmd.lycos.com/content/article/1675.68822
8. Ichiro Kawachi, "Anger and Hostility Linked to Coronary Heart Disease," *Lancet,* www.thelancet.com.
9. Susan Aldridge, "Hostility Is a Major Heart Disease Risk," *Health Psychology,* November 2002.
10. J. C. Barefoot, et al., "Hostility CHD Incidence in Total Mortality—a 25-Year Follow-Up Study of 255 Physicians," *Psychosomatic Medicine,* 45 (1984): 79–83.
11. J. E. Brody, "Why Angry People Can't Control the Short Fuse," *New York Times,* 28 May 2002.
12. R. Eliot, *Is It Worth Dying For?* (NY: Bantam Books, 1984).
13. R. Williams.
14. Meyer Friedman and Ray Rosenman, *Type A Behavior and Your Heart* (New York: Knopf, 1974). See also Ray H. Rosenman, et al., "Coronary Heart Disease in the Western Collaborative Group Study, Final Follow-Up and Follow-Up Experience of 8-1/2 Years," *Journal of the American Medical Association,* 233 (1975): 872–877.
15. Paul Pearsall, *The Heart's Code* (New York: Broadway Books, 1998), 9.

CHAPTER 5

1. J. Sarno, *The Mind-Body* Prescription (NY: Warner Books, 1998).

CHAPTER 6

1. W. E. Narrow, "One-Year Prevalence of Depressive Disorders Among Adults Eighteen and Older in the U.S.," *NIMH ECA Prospective Data.* Population estimates based on U.S. Census estimated residential population age eighteen and over on July 1, 1998. Unpublished.
2. Kiecolt-Glaser, et al., 1998.
3. Pratt, et al., 1996.
4. Frasure-Smith, et al., 1993.
5. Glassman and Shapiro, 1988.
6. Anna Fels, "Mending of Hearts and Minds," *New York Times,* 21 May 2002.
7. Michaels, et al., 1996.
8. Depression Research at the National Institute of Mental Health Office of Communication and Public Liaison, Bethesda, Md., NIH Publication No. 00-4501 (2002).
9. C. J. L. Murray, et al., *Summary: the Global Burden of Disease—A*

*Comprehensive Assessment of Mortality and Disability from Diseases, Injuries and Risk Factors in 1990 and projected to 2020* (Cambridge, Mass.: Harvard University Press, 1996).

10. D. A. Regier, W. E. Narrow, D. S. Rae, et al., "The De Facto Mental and Addictive Disorder Service System: Epidemiologic Catchment Area Prospective One-Year Prevalence Rates of Disorders and Services," *Archives of General Psychiatry,* 50 (1993): 85–94.

11. W. E. Narrow, "One Year Prevalence of Depressive Disorders."

12. D. A. Regier, et al., "The de facto mental and addictive disorders service system. Epidemiologic Cachment Area prospective 1-year prevalence rates of disorders and services."

13. "Understanding the Different Types of Depression," www.Depression-and Anxiety.com, 2002.

14. Martin Seligman, *Learned Optimism* (New York: Pocketbooks, 1998).

15. M. Seligman, *Authentic Happiness* (New York: The Free Press, 2002).

16. Daniel Amen, *Change Your Brain, Change Your Life* (New York: Three Rivers Press, 1998).

17. E. Brounwald, et al., *Harrison's 15 Edition Principles of Internal Medicine* (New York: McGraw-Hill, 2001).

18. R. Sapolsky, *Why Zebras Don't Get Ulcers* (New York: W. H. Freeman and Co., 1999).

19. Depression Research at the National Institute of Mental Health.

20. D. Burns, *Feeling Good* (New York: Avon Books, 1999).

21. G. L. Klerman, et al., "Birth-cohort trends in rates of major depressive disorder among relatives of patients with affective disorder," *Archives of General Psychiatry,* 42 (1985): 689-693.

22. C. Peterson, et al., *Learned Helplessness* (New York: Oxford University Press, 1993).

23. Ibid.

24. Ibid.

CHAPTER 7

1. Pearsall, *The Heart's Code,* 25.

2. Ibid.

3. Pearsall, 27.

4. Ibid., 2.

CHAPTER 8

1. R. Sapolsky, *Why Zebras Don't Get Ulcers* (New York: W. H. Freeman and Co., 1999).

2. Doc Childre, *Overcoming Emotional Chaos* (San Diego, Calif.: Jodere Group, Inc., 2002), 13.

CHAPTER 9

1. J. Borger, "America Remembers," *Guardian Newspaper,* 14 Sept. 2002.

2. W. E. Narrow, et al., NIHM Epidemiology note: "Prevalence of anxiety disorders. One-year prevalence best estimates calculated from ECA and

NCS data. Population estimates based on U.S. Census estimated residential population age 18 to 54 on July 1, 1998."

3. www.achenet.org/understanding.
4. Sabrina Paterniti, et al., "Sustained Anxiety in a Four-Year Progression of Carotid Atherosclerosis," *Arteriosclerosis, Thrombosis and Vascular Biology,*" 36 (2001): 21:136.
5. Allen Rozaniski, et al., "Impact of Psychological Factors and the Pathogenesis of Cardiovascular Disease and Implications for Therapy," *Circulation Period,* 99 (1999): 2192–2217.
6. T. Bruer, et al., "How do clinician practicing in the US manage Heliobacter pylori-related gastrointestinal diseases? *Am J Gastroenterology,* 93 (1998): 553–61.
7. Ibid.
8. W. Salt, *Irritable Bowel Syndrome* (Columbus, Oh.: Parkview Publishing, 1997).
9. S. Cohen, et al., "Psychological Stress and Susceptibility to the Common Cold," *New England Journal of Medicine,* 325 (1991): 606–612.

CHAPTER 10

1. www.datacomm.ch/kmatter/psychone.htmnumber Toc442256827.
2. E. M. Sternberg, et al., "The mind-body interaction in disease," *Scientific American* special issue, 8–15 (1997).
3. Ibid.
4. Ibid.
5. F. Luskin, *Forgive for Good* (New York: HarperCollins, 2002).
6. R.T. Kendall, *Total Forgiveness* (Lake Mary, FL: Charisma House, 2002) .

CHAPTER 11

1. V. E. Frankl, *Man's Search for Meaning* (New York: Washington Press, 1963).
2. J. Armour and J. Ardell, eds., *Neurocardiology* (New York: Oxford University Press, 1984).
3. J. Lacey and B. Lacey, "Some Autonomic-Central Nervous System Interrelationships," found in P. Black, *Physiological Correlates of Emotions* (New York: Academic Press, 1970), 205–275.
4. Jack Frost tape, "The Father's Love."
5. L. Song, G. Schwartz, and L. Russek, "Heart-Focused Attention and Heart-Brain Synchronization: Energetic and Physiological Mechanisms," *Alternative Therapies in Health and Medicine,* 4 (1998): 44–62.
6. Ibid.
7. S. H. Stogtz and I. Stewart, "Coupled Oscillators and Biological Synchronization," *Scientific American,* 269 (1993): 102–109.

CHAPTER 12

1 James V. Durlacher, *Freedom from Fear Forever* (Mesa, Ariz.: Van Ness Publishing Co., 1994), 83–84.
2. Live interview from the American Psychological Association 108th Convention, Washington, D.C., moderator Frank Farley (6 August 2000).

3. A. Beck, et al., *Cognitive Therapy and Depression* (New York: Gilford Press, 1979).
4. David Burns, *Feeling Good* (NY: Harper Collins, 1980).
5. Ibid.

CHAPTER 13

1. Transcript from *Larry King Live*, "Jim and Tammy Faye Return to TV," www.cnn.comtranscripts/0005/29/likl.00.html (May 29, 2000).
2. George Ritchie, *Return from Tomorrow* (Grand Rapids: Baker Book House, 1978), 114–16.
3. W. Tiller, R. McCraty, M. Atkinson, "Toward Cardiac Coherence: A New Noninvasive Measure of Autonomic System Order," *Alternative Therapies*, 2 (1986): 56–65.
4. F.M. Luskin, "The Effect of Forgiveness Training on Psychosocial Factors in College Age Adults," unpublished dissertations (Stanford University, 1999) reported in F. Luskin, *Forgive for Good* (HarperSanFrancisco, 2002), 81–133.
5. Ibid.

CHAPTER 14

1. L. Berk, et al., "Neuroendocrine and stress hormone changes during mirthful laughter," *The American Journal of the Medical Sciences*, 298 (1989): 390–6.
2. C. A. Anderson and L. H. Arnault, "An Examination of Perceived Control, Humor, Irrational Beliefs, and Positive Stress As Moderators of the Relation Between Negative Stress and Health," *Basic and Applied Social Psychology*, 10 (1989): 101–117.
3. Fox, "Looking Forward to a Good Laugh?"
4. W. Cousins "Anatomy of an illness as perceived by the patient," *New England Journal of Medicine*, 295 (1976): 1458–63.
5. "RX Laughter," 31 October 2002, www.rxlaughter.org/press24.html.
6. A. H. Rankin and R. J. Phillip, "Epidemic of Laughter in Bukoba, District of Tanganyika," *Central African Journal of Medicine*, 9 (1963).
7. W. F. Fry, et al., *Make 'Em Laugh* (Palo Alto, Calif.: Science and Behavior Books, 1975).
8. W. Cousins, "Anatomy of all illnesses perceived by the patient."
9. W. F. Fry, *Make 'Em Laugh*.
10. P. Wooten, *Compassionate Laughter* (Salt Lake City, Utah: Commune-A-Key Publishing, 1996).
11. R. Levenson, et al., "Voluntary Facial Action Generates Emotion-Specific Autonomic Nervous System Activity," *Psychophysiology*, 27 (1990): 363–384.
12. Ibid.
13. M. Seligman, *Authentic Happiness* (New York: The Free Press, 2002).
14. L. Harker and D. Keltner, "Expressions of Positive Emotion in Women's College Yearbook Pictures and Their Relationship to Personality and Life Outcomes Across Adulthood," *Journal of Personality and Social Psychology*, 80 (2001): 112–124.

15. L. Gibson, *Laughter, the Universal Language* (New York: Pegasus Expressions, 1990).
16. Seligman.
17. *New York Times.*
18. Seligman.
19. Ibid.
20. G. Vaillant, "Adaptive mental mechanisms: their role in positive psychology," *American Psychologist,* 55 (2000): 89–98.
21. David G. Myers and Ed Diener, "In Pursuit of Happiness," *Scientific American,* May 1996.
22. Seligman.

CHAPTER 15

1 D. Childre, et al., *Overcoming Emotional Chaos.* (San Diego, Calif.: Jodere Group, 2002).
2. E. Jacobson, *Progressive Relaxation* (Chicago: University of Chicago Press, 1938).
3. H. Benson, et al., "The Relaxation Response," *Psychiatry,* 37 (1974): 37–48.
4. M. Hutchison, *The Book of Floating—Exploring the Private Sea* (New York: William Morrow & Co., 1984).
5. V. A. Barnes, "Meditation Decreases Blood Pressure," Center for the Advancement of Health (2 Aug. 1999).
6. H. Koenig, *The Healing Power of Faith* (Touchstone, New York: 1999).
7. J. Baker, *The Bowen Techinique* (Gloucestershire, UK: Corpus Publishing, 2001).
8. "2000 Omnibus Sleep in America Poll," National Sleep Foundation, 1522 (Washington, D.C.).

CHAPTER 16

1. H. Fisher, *The Anatomy of Love* (New York: Fawcett Columbine, 1992).
2. Amanda Onion, "The Science of Love," *ABC News,* 14 February 2001, www.abcnews.go.com/sections/scitech/Holidaysscienceoflov010214.html.
3. Ibid.
4. LSS News, Life Services.com—Internet article.
5. Joanne Tangedahl, *A New Blueprint for Marriage* (Mind and Miracle, 1981).
6. www.adamschocolate.com/chocolate_facts_m.html; Onion, "The Science of Love."
7. Martin Luther King Jr., *The Strength of Love* (Philadelphia: Fortress Press, 1963), 51–52.

# ABOUT THE AUTHOR

Don Colbert, M.D., a board-certified family practitioner since 1987, is the author of such bestsellers as *What Would Jesus Eat, Toxic Relief, Walking in Divine Health,* and the Bible Cure Booklet Series. He writes monthly columns for *Charisma* magazine and Joyce Meyers's *Partners* magazine. Dr. Colbert developed his own vitamin line, Divine Health Nutritional Products, and hosts the national talk show *Your Health Matters,* with his wife Mary. He regularly speaks at national seminars. He makes his home in the Orlando, Florida, area.

# ACKNOWLEDGMENTS

I would like to take a moment to convey my sincerest thanks and appreciation to some very special people who have contributed to my success!

First, I would like to thank Victor Oliver, Mike Hyatt, Ted Squires, and the staff of Thomas Nelson Publishers for believing in me and my work. But most of all for their invaluable support over the years—in my opinion, you are some of God's unseen heroes. Bless you all for helping to spread the Gospel to the world.

I wish to acknowledge Dr. Bill Bright for his courage, peaceful attitude, spirit of gratitude and joy during his journey through life. He finished the race of life with such dignity and grace. "Well, done thy good and faithful servant!" whom I am most confident He heard.

To my partner in life, my wife Mary. A very special "thank you" for your valuable insight and participation in all of my work, and for your love and continued support. You are simply wonderful!

To my parents, who walked with me through my early years sharing their wisdom and love. Thanks for helping me to discover and work on my own "emotions." I will be forever grateful to you both.

There are a host of other people who have lent their support to this project. Without them it would have been nearly impossible. So, I would like to show my appreciation and thanks by taking a moment to acknowledge them: Erin Leigh O'Donnell, my Personal Assistant; Amy Russo, my Physician Assistant; Laural Waltz, my faithful nurse. And to Patti Marden, Sherry Kaiser, and Marci Brooks, for they are my dedicated and hardworking staff.

I wish to also thank Jan Dargatz, Peg de Alminana, Kay Webb, and Beverly Kurtz for their assistance with this publication.

# SALVATION PRAYER

## PRAYER IS TALKING WITH GOD

God knows your heart and is not so concerned with your words as He is with the attitude of your heart. The following is a suggested prayer:

*Lord Jesus, I need You. Thank You for dying on the cross for my sins. I open the door of my life and receive You as my Savior and Lord. Thank You for forgiving my sins and giving me eternal life. Take control of the throne of my life. Make me the kind of person You want me to be.*

Does this prayer express the desire of your heart?

If it does, I invite you to pray this prayer right now, and Christ will come into your life, as He promised.

*How to know that Christ is in your life*

Did you receive Christ into your life? According to His promise in Revelation 3:20, where is Christ right now in relation to you? Christ said that He would come into your life. Would He mislead you? On what authority do you know that God has answered your prayer? (The trustworthiness of God Himself and His Word)

*The Bible promises eternal life for all who receive Christ.*

"The witness is this, that God has given us eternal life, and this life is in His Son. He who has the Son has the life; he who does not have the Son of God does not have the life. These things I have written to you who believe in the name of the Son of God, in order that you may know that you have eternal life" (1 John 5:11). Thank God often that Christ is in your life and that He will never leave you (Hebrews 13:5). You can know on the basis of His promise that Christ lives in you and that you have eternal life from the very moment you invite Him in. He will not deceive you!

## LAW #1
God *loves* you and offers a wonderful *plan* for your life.

*God's Love:* "God so loved the world that He gave His one and only Son, that whoever believes in Him shall not perish but have eternal life" (John 3:16, NIV).

## LAW #2
Man is *sinful* and *separated* from God. Therefore, he cannot know and experience God's love and plan for his life.

*Man Is Sinful:* "All have sinned and fall short of the glory of God" (Romans 3:23).
*Man Is Separated:* "The wages of sin is death" [spiritual separation from God] (Romans 6:23).

## LAW #3
Jesus Christ is God's *only* provision for man's sin. Through Him you can know and experience God's love and plan for your life.

*He Died in Our Place:* "God demonstrates His own love toward us, in that while we were yet sinners, Christ died for us (Romans 5:8).
*He Is the Only Way to God.* "Jesus said to him, 'I am the way, and the truth and the life; no one comes to the Father but through Me (John 14:6).

## LAW #4
We must individually *receive* Jesus Christ as Savior and Lord;
then we can know and experience God's love
and plan for our lives.

*We Must Receive Christ:* "As many as received Him, to them He gave the right to become children of God, even those who believe in His name (John 1:12).

*We Receive Christ Through Personal Invitation:* [Christ speaking] "Behold, I stand at the door and knock; if any one hears My voice and opens the door, I will come to him" (Revelation 3:20).

Written by Bill Bright, Campus Crusade for Christ (Orlando, FL: NewLife Publications. 1994).

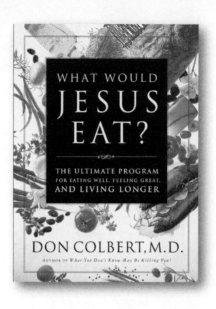

What if there were an "owners manual" for the human body
that came straight from the original manufacturer?
Well, here it is—the first eating guide based on God's teaching
and Jesus' example. *In What Would Jesus Eat?*, best-selling
author Dr. Don Colbert confirms: "The medical facts are in. If we
eat as Jesus ate, we will be healthier."
Living as the perfect role model, Jesus wisely consumed whole-
grain breads, pure water, and fresh foods that were low in fat,
salt, additives, and preservatives. His diet proves flawless even in
the twenty-first century with all its expanded food choices—
they simply do not offer the nutrition Jesus' diet does.
Whether you want to lose weight, prevent disease,
eat more balanced meals, attain vibrant health, or adopt a diet
designed with biblical authority,
*What Would Jesus Eat?* is for you.

**Book ISBN: 0-7852-6567-8**

**Cookbook ISBN: 0-7852-6519-8**

**Audio ISBN: 0-7852-6598-8**

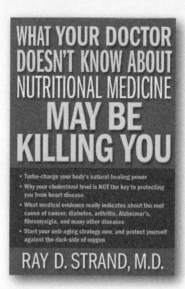

WHAT YOUR DOCTOR
DOESN'T KNOW ABOUT
NUTRITIONAL MEDICINE
MAY BE
KILLING YOU

• Turbo-charge your body's natural healing power
• Why your cholesterol level is NOT the key to protecting you from heart disease
• What medical evidence really indicates about the root cause of cancer, diabetes, arthritis, Alzheimer's, fibromyalgia, and many other diseases
• Start your anti-aging strategy *now*, and protect yourself against the *dark-side* of oxygen

RAY D. STRAND, M.D.

When Dr. Ray Strand found himself in a losing battle, unable to successfully treat his wife who had suffered chronically with pain and fatigue, he agreed to have her try the regimen of nutritional supplements that a neighbor suggested.

Much to his surprise, his wife's condition began to improve almost immediately, and now she enjoys a full life with excellent health. That amazing turn of events led him to dedicate himself to researching alternative therapies in medicine, particularly in the arena of nutritional supplements.

Dr. Strand's illumination of the body's silent enemy—oxidative stress—will astound you. But, more importantly, his research will equip you to protect or reclaim your nutritional health, possibly reversing disease and preventing illness.

ISBN: 0-7852-6486-8